Autism

Autism

by ELAINE LANDAU

FRANKLIN WATTS

A Division of Scholastic Inc.
New York / Toronto / London / Auckland / Sydney
Mexico City / New Delhi / Hong Kong
Danbury, Connecticut

For Jocelyn Kessler

Photographs ©: AP/Wide World Photos: 48 (Kelly J. Huff/The Daily Ledger), 112 (Tyler Mallory), 49 (Douglas C. Pizac), 106 (Don Ryan), 101 (Richard Gwin/Lawrence Journal World); Corbis-Bettmann: 70 (Alex Gotfryd), 40 (UPI), 36; Liaison Agency, Inc.: 67 (Francois Scheitzer/SAOLA), 109 (Lawrence Schwartzwald); Photo Researchers, NY: 42 (John Bavosi/SPL), 47 (Will & Deni McIntyre), 20, 72, 76, (Nancy Pierce), 16 (Ellen B. Senisi); PhotoEdit/David Young-Wolff: 8; Stone/Patrick Molnar: cover; The Image Works: 23, 26, 52 (Alan Carey), 29 (Jim Pickerell), 10, 28, 54 (Ellen B. Senisi); TRIP Photo Library/H. Rogers: 12.

Book production by Editorial Directions
Interior design by Molly Heron

Library of Congress Cataloging-in-Publication Data

Landau, Elaine.
    Autism / Elaine Landau.
    p. cm.
    Includes bibliographical references and index.
    ISBN 0-531-11780-4
1. Autism—Juvenile literature. 2. Autism in children—Juvenile literature.
[1. Autism. 2. Mentally handicapped.] I. Title.

RC553.A88 L364 2001
6216.89'82—dc21   00-042643

Contents

CHAPTER ONE

Kevin Wasn't Like His Brothers

WHEN HE WAS $2\frac{1}{2}$ years old, Kevin wasn't like his brothers were at that age. He didn't speak, or look directly at you when you spoke to him. His parents and brothers were never quite sure that he understood what they were saying. Also, Kevin didn't like to be touched. Once, when a well-meaning neighbor grabbed Kevin to give him a hug, he shrieked loudly and ran to the other side of the room.

Sometimes it seemed as if Kevin lived in his own world—a world that those around him could not enter or even understand. Kevin would sit for hours carefully examining one or two toys that he always kept near him. Other times during the day he would sit on the floor clutching himself while rocking back and forth.

Because they have difficulty communicating, autistic children sometimes have tantrums.

Kevin's temper tantrums were especially difficult for his family to deal with. His limited language skills made communication hard. It was obvious that when Kevin could not make those around him understand his wants or needs he became extremely frustrated. This resulted in frequent screaming outbursts. One of his brothers joked that he didn't want to be in the room when Kevin was angry, adding that he'd prefer not to be hit in the head by whatever Kevin might throw.

Kevin's parents did not want to think that something was wrong with their little boy. They told themselves that Kevin was merely going through "the terrible twos" and that all two-year-olds were sometimes hard to handle. They also knew that little boys sometimes develop language skills later than girls and reasoned that was why Kevin failed to speak. Though both these things were true, Kevin represented an extreme. He wasn't like his brothers or like any other two-year-old his parents had ever seen.

In the months ahead, Kevin would visit a number of doctors. The toddler's hearing was tested. Because someone could walk into the room and say hello to Kevin without his even looking up, there was the possibility that his hearing was severely impaired. But that was soon ruled out, as were a number of other conditions.

In the end, Kevin's family learned that they would be facing a serious challenge in the years ahead. They would be bringing up a child who had been diagnosed as autistic.

Autism is not a disease—no one can "catch" autism. It is a developmental disorder that affects how a person's brain functions. Its symptoms usually appear sometime during a child's first three years. At times, parents of autistic children claim that they knew something was wrong right away. Some autistic babies cry incessantly and nothing their parents or caregivers do to comfort them seems to help. At other times, autistic infants are unusually quiet.

One mother of an autistic child noted that her baby did not seem to crave attention the way other infants did. He was content to lie alone in his crib and cried only if he was hungry or soaking wet. Her neighbor tried to tell her that he was just a "good baby," but the child's mother sensed early on that this infant was "too good to be true" and was not responding to her or to his environment the way a typical baby would.

Autistic children can have trouble focusing their attention on other people.

As the months passed, the child resisted being held or cuddled. He could not be engaged in play and seemed unaffected by his parents' smiles or other facial expressions. While most babies delight in a game of peekaboo, autistic babies frequently turn away. They seem to purposely avoid eye contact with those around them. Their parents later learn that this behavior is common in children with the disorder.

Other parents have very different experiences. Their children appear to develop normally during the first 18 to 20 months of life. Many enjoy being held by their parents and interacting with other family members as babies. These young children also seem to be learning to speak, but may "lose" their words before they turn three. In some instances, toddlers who are able to say about 20 words just seem to forget them rather than continue adding to their vocabulary. There are often personality changes, too, as young children start to withdraw more into themselves.

Both boys and girls can be autistic but the disorder is much more common in boys. Autism strikes males about four times more often than females, so four out of every five autistic children are likely to be boys. Yet anyone can be autistic. People around the world have been diagnosed with this disorder. It knows no racial or ethnic boundaries, and it affects people of all income and educational levels. Autistic children can be found in both wealthy and poor families. A college professor is as likely to have an autistic child as someone who never completed elementary school.

The general signs of autism frequently appear in early childhood and can continue throughout the person's life.

A school for autistic children in Kuwait

At present, there is no cure for autism. However, treatments are available that, in many cases, help to curb undesirable behaviors. The National Institute of Mental Health (NIMH), a division of the National Institutes of Health (NIH), is the federal government's primary agency for biomedical and behavioral research. NIMH notes that autism affects from 1 to 2 of every 1,000 people.[1] When people with disorders similar to autism are included in these estimates, the numbers may be two to three times greater, however.

In addition to the tremendous loss of human potential caused by the disorder, those affected need health and educational services amounting to more than $3 billion annually. Therefore, in one way or another, autism affects us all. This is a book about autism, a disorder that has challenged the mental health community for decades.

CHAPTER TWO

The Signs of Autism

AUTISM AFFECTS PEOPLE differently. Often there is a great deal of variation in symptoms. It's impossible to describe someone with autism and say that all autistic individuals are like that. Some people are more severely affected than others. In the worst instances, the symptoms persist over time and prove extremely difficult to change. Such individuals pose a tremendous challenge to their parents, doctors, and teachers. On the other hand, people with very mild forms of autism often have a considerably easier time adjusting to society's norms and expectations.

However, to be diagnosed with autism, affected individuals usually show some degree of the following symptoms.

PROBLEMS WITH SOCIAL BEHAVIOR

Children with autism do not respond to people and situations the way other children do. Parents of autistic children often feel that their babies are not emotionally attached to them. As one mother put it, "I am only important to him as the one who fulfills his needs. If it were not me, then it could just as well be a total stranger."[1]

Autistic babies do not crave physical contact the way other babies do. They don't enjoy being picked up and cuddled and will not nestle against the person holding them as most babies do. Instead of stretching out their arms and smiling when a parent or caregiver comes to hold them, these babies have been known to cry when approached. One mother described what it was like as follows:

"He hated to be held—he'd squirm and arch his back. He didn't look at me or Donald [her husband]. He cried every night until 5 A.M. He was constantly sick. When he didn't talk by 18 months, I worried, but everyone said, 'Oh well, kids develop differently.'"[2] She later learned that it was more than that—her son was autistic.

Another mother told her pediatrician that she had a terrible time getting her baby to eat. When she held her young son comfortably against her to give him his bottle of formula, the baby rebelled. He would cry, struggle to free himself, and spit up much of the formula. It was clear early on that mealtimes while he was in his mother's arms were high-stress periods.

Ironically, the child's mother stumbled on a solution when she came down with a bad case of the flu. To

15

A girl tries to engage her autistic classmate.

avoid exposing the baby to infection, she propped up his bottle on a pillow so that that the child could have his formula without being held. To her astonishment, the struggle seemed to be over. The baby drank the formula and for the first time almost seemed to enjoy it. When the mother recovered and went back to holding her son while feeding him, he appeared upset and behaved as he formerly had. It was obvious that the little boy was more at ease when he was not in his mother's arms.

As autistic children grow, their lack of attachment to their parents and others around them may become increasingly noticeable. In playgroups or day care, their behavior frequently differs markedly from that of the other children. Autistic children tend to be loners. In fact, the word *autism* comes from *autos*, a Greek word meaning "self."

Autistic children are most often seen playing quietly by themselves. They may become completely absorbed in an activity they've latched onto. At times, it is almost as if they are unaware of the other children in the room. Even with a group of loud playful children circling them, the autistic youngster may not even look around to see what they are up to. Such behavior was especially obvious in the case study of an autistic boy named Peter.

"When Peter joined a play group of toddlers his age, the differences between him and the other children became impossible to ignore. He did not appear to notice the other children. He always played alone... Peter moved around quietly collecting all of the stuffed animals into a pile.

"Peter's parents suspected that he was deaf [because

he seemed so unaware of the commotion in the room] and asked their pediatrician for a referral to a specialist."[3] As it turned out, there was nothing wrong with their son's hearing.

Peter's case is not uncommon. Parents of autistic children often think their offspring might be hearing impaired because these children frequently may seem oblivious to the noisy activities surrounding them. Such children tend to resist taking part in games involving other children. When they do, they usually remain passive participants rather than becoming actively involved. At times, the closest an autistic child comes to being part of a game is standing on the sidelines watching the other children. A neurologist visiting a school for autistic children described what things were like on the playground:

"At one such school as I approached, I had seen some children in the playground, swinging and playing ball. How normal I thought—but when I got closer I saw one child swinging obsessively in terrifying semicircles, as high as the swing would go; another throwing a small ball from hand to hand; another spinning on a roundabout, around and around; another not building with bricks but lining them up endlessly, in neat, monotonous rows. All were engaged in solitary, repetitive activities; none was really playing, or playing with any of the others."[4]

Those who have worked with autistic children note that some frequently treat other people as though they were inanimate objects. For example, such a child might climb up on his father's lap to reach a toy truck on a high shelf. But he doesn't smile or acknowledge his father's role while doing so. This is not a playful or

18

fun exercise designed to both get the truck and be closer to his dad. For him, it's as if there is no difference between standing on his father or on a chair to get the truck.

Autistic children don't recognize the more subtle cues from others that help us gauge our behavior. They may know when a parent is furious, but a disapproving look is lost on them. Missing the less obvious hints leading to what is expected of them makes it even more difficult for an autistic child to meet the expectations of others. The autistic child is not sensitive to the feelings of those around him. They seem to "tune out" and are completely unaware that someone may be hurt or frustrated by their actions or lack of response.

SPEECH AND LANGUAGE DIFFICULTIES

Autistic children are slow to develop language skills. This slowness to speak generally becomes a serious concern of the child's parents and frequently leads to a barrage of medical tests to rule out a number of possible conditions. Some autistic children never learn to talk. They may point or grunt to indicate to others what they want. At times they will lead a parent or teacher over to an object and place that person's hand on it.

Sixteen-year-old Michael is very intelligent, but because of his autism he has never spoken a word. Yet he manages to communicate with his family. As his mother described it, "When Michael was eight, he took an antibiotic out of the refrigerator, then brought it to me and pointed to his ear. Sure enough, he had an ear infection."[5] If the family is eating out, Michael casts his vote for the restaurant of his choice by pointing to a matchbook with the establishment's name on the cover. He has also learned to make his needs known by using a stack of picture cards.

Autistic individuals who talk may not speak as most people do. According to the National Institute of Mental Health, "Those who speak often use language in unusual ways. Some seem unable to combine words into meaningful sentences. Some speak only single words. Others repeat the same phrase no matter what the situation."[6]

Often, autistic children who speak merely repeat what they've heard. This condition is known as echolalia. As the name suggests, they echo or repeat what is said to them. So if someone said to an autistic

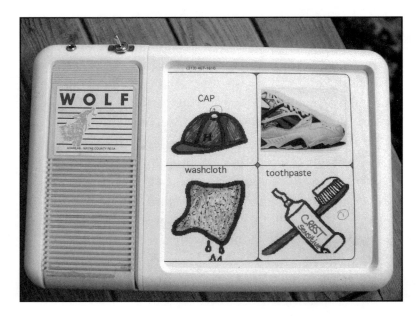

A Wolf board is used by autistic people to communicate. When someone touches a picture, an electronic voice says the word.

child, "Do you want to go bowling?" the child might respond by repeating the question, "Do you want to go bowling?" instead of answering yes or no. While having whatever you say to someone repeated back to you can be quite annoying, the child is not doing it to be provocative.

Besides immediate echolalia—repeating what has been said to them right away—people with autism often also display delayed echolalia. This can entail repeating an entire conversation that took place over a week ago or the words to a television commercial they saw several days earlier.

Some autistic children will repeat the same phrase for a variety of circumstances. For example, a child may say, "Close the door," several times throughout the day. To the listener who sees that the door is already closed, the request may seem senseless. Yet the child may actually be saying "Close the door" to indicate that he or she wants to go outside. In the child's mind, the phrase "close the door" has become associated with leaving the house.

In a similar instance a 10-year-old autistic boy became quite upset when his brother accidentally broke a jar containing a sugar and cinnamon mixture that he liked on buttered toast. His mother related what happened this way: "Trying to deescalate his tension, which I knew could easily grow into a full-scale tantrum, I tried unsuccessfully to find an exact replica of the broken jar. He had a very difficult time accepting the mixture in a different container . . . but gradually settled down. Then he said, more to himself than us, 'The Sunoco station is a library.' Knowing the context I was amazed at what he had figured out. An abandoned gas station down the street had been recently turned into a library. He did not have the words to say, 'It's okay to use a different jar.' Instead he had to use an analogy, with the words we had used many times to talk about the transformation of the gas station. That change had bothered him for weeks. The building was no longer a 'container' for the Sunoco gas station. Its exterior was now made to look like a library. Others who do not know him, or do not share his experience, or do not know autism well, could easily have labeled his explanation to himself as 'garbage talk' or 'autistic nonsense'."[7]

At times, autistic children who feel frustrated at not being able to communicate may scream or simply reach out and grab an item. As one autistic woman who made remarkable strides in life later wrote of her early lack of language, "Not being able to speak was utter frustration. Screaming was the only way I could communicate." In some situations she would say to herself, "I am going to scream now because I want to tell somebody I don't want to do something."[8] Such behavior is the autistic individual's way of coping in a world where language can be a barrier.

The speech of autistic people is often described as "uniform" or "monotone." That means that it lacks expression. In monotonic speech, it is difficult to detect joy, sadness, or any other emotion. In some cases, an autistic person's speech may sound mechanical or robotlike. Other autistic individuals speak in a high-pitched voice.

The language of autistic children frequently includes pronoun reversal. In speaking about themselves, these children will say "you" instead of "I."

A speech pathologist working with a group of autistic students

They also often refer to themselves by their name instead of saying "I."

In addition, autistic people who speak may experience problems conversing appropriately with others. They often find it hard to select a topic of interest to the listener or may begin all their conversations by asking for the person's address or something equally bizarre. At times, an autistic person's idea of a conversation may be delivering a monologue (a short speech) on something that interests him or her but not necessarily the person being spoken to. These autistic individuals can speak in depth on a particular subject, such as airplanes, but may not be able to engage in a two-way conversation on the topic.

Autistic individuals also tend to take whatever is said literally. They are often unable to understand generalities or common expressions in speech. This is well illustrated by the following case study that shows a five year-old autistic boy's problems in learning his therapist's name:

"For some reason he [the boy] kept calling the therapist 'Poster.' Finally, after several frustrating attempts to have the child use his correct name, the therapist said, 'Kenny, my name is not Poster!' A few minutes later when asked the therapist's name, the child answered, 'Not Poster!' In fact, the child referred to him as "'Not Poster' ever after."[9]

INAPPROPRIATELY RESPONDING TO THEIR SURROUNDINGS

An autistic child may have unusual responses to sound, touch, or other sensory stimulation. As the National Institute of Mental Health described it, "When children's perceptions are accurate, they can learn from what they see, feel, or hear. On the other hand, if sensory information is faulty or if the input from the various senses fails to merge into a coherent picture, the child's experiences of the world can be confusing. People with autism seem to have one or both of these problems. . . . Apparently as a result of brain malfunction, many children with autism are highly attuned, or even painfully sensitive, to certain sounds, textures, tastes, and smells."[10]

A child who may not look up from whatever he's doing when a car loudly backfires only a few feet away may cover his ears and run screaming from a room at the sound of a clock ticking or a door being quietly closed. One young autistic boy showed his aversion to being touched when a doctor with a stethoscope came toward him to examine him. An observer described the boy's reaction as follows:

"When the attending physician approached him with his stethoscope, the little boy began to moan—no, not moan exactly. It was more like an expression of discomfort, a sound I had never heard come from a child. The doctor had not even touched him yet.

"When the stethoscope was finally pressed to the boy's chest, his moan became a wild, desperate shriek of pain. His mother held him tightly, barely able to restrain the tiny, suddenly terrified child. When the physician slipped away from the boy, he immediately quieted. Still anxious, he jumped from his mother's lap and toward the examination-room door. It was closed. This seemed to add to his frustration."[11]

A well-functioning autistic woman described how she felt affected as a child this way: "The school bell was like a dentist's drill down my ear," she recalled. She went on to note that the petticoat beneath her dress felt like "sandpaper rubbing off my skin." Living in the everyday environment most people regard as normal gave her "a constant feeling like I was being mugged in New York City. . . . If you had a speaker inside of you blaring rock-and-roll with a psychedelic light show, you'd withdraw too," she added.[12]

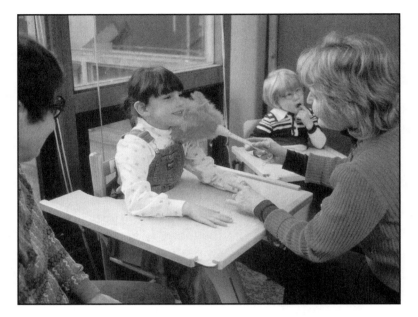

A feather tickle is a pleasant reward for this autistic child.

Many autistic children also have a reduced sensitivity to pain. Some autistic children will barely notice a bruise or cut from a fall that might cause most young children to cry. Yet the same child can be extraordinarily sensitive to other sensations. Some autistic children cannot stand to be touched and their intense resistance to being cuddled is a characteristic of the disorder.

REPETITIVE BEHAVIORS AND OBSESSIONS

Autistic children frequently engage in repetitive behaviors at various times throughout the day. This may include rocking, hand-flapping, hair-twirling, tensing their muscles, and waving their hands and fingers in front of their faces. Some also engage in self-injurious behavior such as biting themselves or banging their heads against a wall. Many autistic children have a particular fascination with objects that spin. They may spend hours a day spinning the wheels on a toy truck or the lid of a pot. "Scientists are exploring several possible explanations for such repetitive, obsessive behavior," the NIMH explained. "Perhaps the order and sameness lends some stability in a world of sensory confusion. Perhaps focused behavior helps them to block out painful stimuli. Yet another theory is that behaviors are linked to the senses that work well or poorly. A child who sniffs everything in sight may be using a stable sense of smell to explore his environment. Or perhaps the reverse is true; he may be trying to stimulate a sense that is dim."[13]

Autistic children are frequently inflexible. They often insist on certain rituals or routines and become extremely upset when these are interrupted. Some autistic children will eat only certain foods prepared in a specific way or served in a predefined order. One little girl would eat only oranges cut in quarters and peanut butter and jelly sandwiches made with grape jelly. If the orange was peeled instead of quartered or if the sandwich had strawberry jelly instead of grape jelly, the child would push the food away and scream. This need not to have their routines disturbed may extend to other aspects of the autistic person's life. These individuals may become extremely distressed if the furniture in their room is rearranged or if their parent takes a different route driving them home.

The play of autistic children tends to be unimaginative and often reflects this need for sameness. The

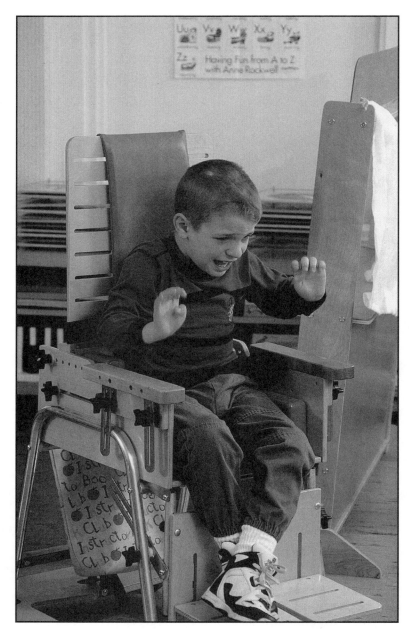

Repetitive banging is a common trait of autism.

NIMH described how an autistic child's play differs from that of other young people as follows: "[The autistic child's] imaginative play, too, is limited by these repetitive behaviors and obsessions. Most children, as early as two, use their imagination to pretend. They create new uses for an object, perhaps using a bowl for a hat. Or they pretend to be someone else, like a mother cooking dinner for her 'family' of dolls. In contrast, children with autism rarely pretend. Rather than rocking a doll, or rolling a toy car, they may simply hold it, smell it, or spin it for hours on end."[14]

One young autistic boy collected about 10 paper

Most young children participate in imaginary play, such as pretending to be doctors.

clips from around his house. He treasured them—taking the clips with him wherever he went. Often during the day, he would line the paper clips up in a row on the kitchen table. Though his mother put out other potentially more exciting toys for her son to play with, he continued to ignore them in favor of the clips.

In the chart below,[15] the NIMH summarized the differences in the behaviors of very young children with and without autism. However, while these behaviors may be present initially, at times autistic symptoms improve with treatment, or even as a child simply grows older.

Infants with Autism	Normal Infants
Communication	
Avoid eye contact	Study mother's face
Seem deaf	Easily stimulated by sounds
Start developing language, then abruptly stop talking altogether.	Keep adding to vocabulary and expanding grammatical usage.
Social Relationships	
Act as if unaware of the coming and going of others.	Cry when mother leaves the room and are anxious with strangers.
Physically attack and injure others without provocation.	Get upset when hungry or frustrated.
Inaccessible, as if in a shell.	Recognize familiar faces and smile.

Exploration of Environment

Remain fixated on a single item or activity.	Move from one engrossing activity to another.
Practice strange actions like rocking or hand-flapping.	Use body purposefully to reach or acquire objects.
Sniff or lick toys.	Explore and play with toys.
Show no sensitivity to burns or bruises, engage in self-mutilation, such as eye gouging.	Seek pleasure and avoid pain.

Courtesy NIMH

Although at one time most people with autism were believed to have normal or above-normal intelligence, the current data indicate that this may not be so. The National Institute of Neurological Disorders and Stroke of the NIH cites that the majority of autistic individuals are mentally retarded. The Institute reports: "About half of the people with autism score below 50 on IQ tests, 20 percent score between 50 and 70 and 30 percent score higher than 70."[16] A score under 70 indicates mild retardation. Obtaining accurate IQ scores for autistic children, however, can be extremely difficult. Many professionals indicate that behavior and language problems often interfere with testing.

Autism is called a spectrum disorder because its symptoms and characteristics vary greatly from person to person. This means that autistic behaviors span a broad range, or spectrum. These differences often result in the varied diagnoses outlined here. The conditions described are known as autism spectrum disorders:

Pervasive Developmental Disorder (PDD)—Frequently, children exhibiting some of the symptoms of autism but not enough to be diagnosed with the disorder in its classic form are said to have PDD.

Asperger's Syndrome—This term is sometimes used to describe individuals with autistic behaviors whose early language skills developed on time. In many, there were no delays in intellectual development either. The symptoms of Asperger's Syndrome tend to be identified later in childhood than those of autism.

Childhood Disintegrative Disorder—This diagnosis is frequently applied to children who seemed completely normal for at least their first two years of life. After that, they began to lose their acquired skills and started to show autistic behaviors.

Rett's Disorder—Rett's Disorder affects only females. It is characterized by inadequate brain growth, seizures, and other neurological problems in addition to autistic behaviors.

Arriving at a diagnosis of autism can be tricky. No simple medical test exists to determine if someone has the disorder. X rays and blood tests do not detect it. The diagnosis must be based on a professional observation of the person's language skills, behavior, and level of interpersonal development. While there is no test for autism, various medical tests are usually given to rule out other conditions with similar symptoms.

Ideally, a team of specialists should work with the

child before a diagnosis is arrived at. Because autistic behavior can be so varied, two people with the disorder may act very differently. Therefore it's useful for a multidisciplinary team to help evaluate the patient. Those involved should include a neurologist, psychologist, pediatrician, speech therapist, and learning consultant.

Seeing the patient only once for a brief period often will not provide adequate input to arrive at a correct diagnosis. Additional information from parents or caregivers can offer helpful clues and will fill in gaps. A correct diagnosis is vital if the young person is to be given an effective treatment and educational plan.

The Autism Society of America notes that more than half a million people in the United States today either have autism or one of the related disorders. It's a serious problem that deserves our attention and resources.

CHAPTER THREE

A Historical View of Autism

MANY NEUROLOGICAL DISORDERS have a long history of investigation and treatment but autism was not identified until 1943. A doctor at Johns Hopkins University in Baltimore named Leo Kanner isolated it through his work with a group of 11 children whose symptoms did not fit any existing diagnosis. Yet all these children shared a number of behavioral characteristics—signs that would eventually be recognized as the symptoms of autism. As Kanner noted in his 1943 paper, "Autistic Disturbances of Affective Contact":

"Since 1938 there have come to our attention a number of children whose condition differs so markedly and uniquely from anything reported so far, that each case merits—and, I hope will eventually receive—a detailed consideration of its fascinating peculiarities."[1]

Many of the characteristics Kanner described, such as social isolation, language problems, and insistence on adhering to routines and rituals, have become the hallmarks of autism. But even though autism wasn't recognized as a disorder until 1943, people had suffered with its symptoms for centuries. Often these individuals were labeled as "stupid" or "crazy" or both.

Today, it's strongly suspected that a boy named Victor who became famous as the Wild Boy of Aveyron in 1801 was probably autistic. The story began in the late 1700s when residents of the French village of Aveyron glimpsed what appeared to be a wild boy darting through the surrounding woods. This naked child was also spotted scavenging in the area for roots and acorns to eat. At the sight of other humans, he would quickly dart off into the forest. However, in September 1799, three sportsmen venturing into the woods captured the boy as he tried to escape by scampering up a tree.

The men returned to the village with a child about 11 or 12 years old whose body was covered with scars and who appeared "wild" in every sense of the word. He had obviously fended for himself for years in the forest. He could not speak but raged and spat when cornered. Obviously never having seen a toilet, the youth urinated and defecated wherever he stood.

It was immediately clear that this "wild child," as he was referred to, felt intensely uncomfortable around other people and it wasn't long before he escaped from the home of a widow in whose care he'd been placed. For the next 2 ½ months, the boy roamed local mountain ranges. Though he wore only a thin shirt he'd been given, he appeared able to tolerate the cold easily.

After being captured for the second time, the boy was taken to Paris for scientific observation. At the time, no one had ever heard of autism. Yet the child displayed a number of autistic behaviors. He rocked and swayed back and forth throughout much of the day. Communication was largely impossible—at best he would grunt or make unintelligible sounds in response to nothing in particular. Though numerous people approached him at various times, he seemed indifferent to those around him. His interactions were limited to trying to bite or scratch the people attempting to care for him.

Philippe Pinel, a well-known French educator and

French psychologist Philippe Pinel

psychologist, was called in to examine the boy. He found that the youth could not distinguish between a real object and one in a picture. He also noted other characteristics that would much later be considered indicative of autism. Pinel observed that the boy had not minded being out in the bitter cold while wandering in the mountains—many autistic children either overreact or underreact to extremes in temperature. He also saw that odors had no effect on the boy. The child's reaction and facial expression did not vary whether he was smelling an expensive French perfume or sniffing his own excrement. Autistic individuals are often either oblivious or highly sensitive to such stimuli.

Pinel concluded that the child they called Victor was mentally retarded. However, at the time, a 26-year-old physician named Jean-Marc Itard hesitated to believe the renowned specialist. Itard eagerly accepted the task of working with Victor, hoping to prove that the child was not retarded but that the unruly boy's actions were the result of growing up without human contact. Itard would try to fill in the gaps in young Victor's life by taking him into his home and working closely with him.

After spending some time with the boy, however, Itard had realized that this was not going to be as easy as he had initially thought. Although he didn't know it at the time, much of Victor's behavior precisely fit the present-day criteria for autism. After being with Victor for a while, Itard summarized the boy's existence as largely consisting of "sleeping, eating, doing nothing, and running about the fields."[2]

Like Pinel and others who had observed Victor,

Itard could not help but notice the boy's indifference to cold and heat. Before he could be stopped, Victor would run out half naked to play in the newly fallen snow. If left to do as he pleased, the boy would remain outside for hours rolling around in the snow and even enthusiastically munching on fistfuls of it. As with many autistic individuals, the same indifference to sensation applied to extreme heat. Victor would readily pick up a coal or potato from the fire and not look as if he were doing anything out of the ordinary.

Another autistic characteristic was Victor's lack of interest in creative or imaginative play. He refused to play with any of the toys purchased for him and even threw a set of bowling pins Itard had thought he might like into the fire. Though Victor eventually learned to say one or two words, he never understood their meaning and remained completely oblivious to the language of others around him. At best, he learned to use a few simple gestures to make his needs known.

After about five years, Itard gave up on Victor. He reasoned that Victor was mentally retarded as Dr. Pinel had said. He felt that the child might have been abandoned in the woods as a toddler when his family realized that he was not like other children. Today, mental-health specialists reviewing Victor's case and others like his through the years realize that he wasn't just mentally retarded. He was probably autistic as well.

Dr. Leo Kanner's work in identifying autism was essential to those working with autistic children. Yet Kanner wasn't completely on target regarding all aspects of the disorder. This was largely a result of the small number of children he worked with as well as the absence of other research at that time.

Kanner believed that autistic children tended to be of average or above-average intelligence. This was later found to be untrue. A large percentage of autistic children proved to be at least mildly retarded. Kanner also wrongly argued that poor parenting was a factor in autism. He thought that the parents of autistic children lacked warmth, causing these young people to retreat into themselves.

For the most part, Kanner viewed the parents of autistic children as highly intelligent but largely unavailable emotionally. Relying on the criteria set forth by Kanner, *Time* magazine once described autistic children as being "the offspring of highly organized professional parents, cold and rational . . . [who] just happened to defrost long enough to produce a child."[3] The famous psychoanalyst Bruno Bettelheim further advanced this essentially incorrect theory of the parent being the problem in autism. Bettelheim was convinced that autism occurred as the result of the child's withdrawal from the hostile and forbidding environment the parents presented.

Research through the years has shown these theories to be grossly inaccurate. Poor parenting does not cause autism. Many parents of autistic children have other children with no sign of the disorder. Today, we know that autistic children did not become the way they are because they were unwanted, neglected, or ignored. On the contrary, in many instances the parents of autistic children have tried hard to include these young people in family activities. Yet, because of past false information, many parents have been seen as responsible for

Psychiatrist Dr. Bruno Bettelheim incorrectly blamed autism on poor parenting.

causing this disorder. In an effort to give people accurate information, the Autism Society of America has tried to clarify precisely what autism is *not*. It states: "Autism is *not* a mental illness. Children with autism are *not* unruly kids who choose *not* to behave. . . . Furthermore, no known psychological factors in the development of the child have been shown to cause autism."[4]

Meanwhile researchers throughout the world continue to search for clues to the causes of autism. At this time, no single cause has been identified but the evidence points to probable biological or neurological differences in the brain of autistic individuals. Some data indicate that people with autism may have abnormalities in several regions of their brain. In these regions, neurons—nerve cells in the brain that process information—seem smaller than normal. These neurons also have stunted nerve fibers that may interfere with nerve signaling within the brain. Some believe that these abnormalities suggest that autism results from a disruption of normal brain development while the fetus is still in the womb.

Different theories indicate that other abnormalities in the brain may be responsible for the disorder. These may be problems related to serotonin (a chemical that transmits nerve impulses or signals between neurons) or other signaling molecules in the brain. According to the National Organization for Rare Disorders, "Several of the defects in autism can be traced to the central nervous system's lack of ability to process and respond to informational input, particularly hearing (auditory) and seeing (visual) stimuli."[5]

In attempting to explain what causes autism, the

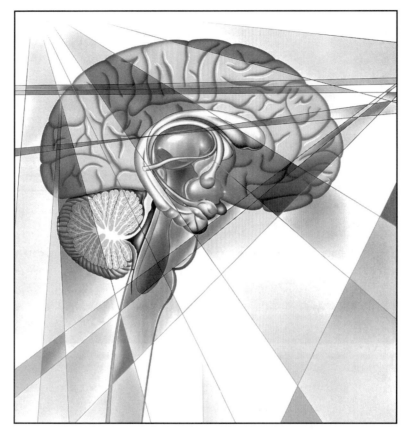

The limbic system, located in the center of the brain, is a network of nerve pathways that govern instinct and mood.

National Institute of Mental Health cites that: "Scientists are also looking for abnormalities in the brain structures that make up the limbic system. Inside the limbic system, an area called the amygdala is known to help regulate aspects of social and emotional behavior. One study of high-functioning children with autism found that the amygdala was indeed impaired. . . . Scientists [have also studied] the development of monkeys whose amygdala was disrupted at birth. Like [autistic] children . . . as the monkeys grew they became increasingly withdrawn and avoided social contact."[6]

In a small number of cases, medical conditions such as congenital rubella and untreated phenylketonuria (PKU) among others may cause autistic behavior. PKU is a progressive metabolic disorder affecting infants. Congenital rubella can occur when a pregnant woman contracts German measles and the virus is transmitted to the fetus. It is also possible that other viruses affecting neurons in the fetal brain can cause autism.

Many people believe that genetics may play a role in autism. The disorder seems to run in some families. Scientists note that parents who have one autistic child are more likely than the rest of the population to have a second autistic child. When one identical twin is autistic, the other usually is too.

Some work has been done on isolating the genes that might make some infants susceptible to autism. Interestingly, in families with an autistic child, other family members sometimes demonstrate mild autistic-like symptoms that still permit them to function normally but nevertheless may be linked to the disorder. It is also statistically true that in families where somebody is autistic there is a higher incidence of emotional disorders such as manic depression and other related conditions. While no specific gene has been linked to autism as yet, work in this area is ongoing. Autism's genetic basis may prove to involve a combination of several genes.

At times, other problems such as learning disabilities, attention deficit disorder, and Tourette's syndrome can also be present with autism. However, while these conditions may occur with autism, they do not cause it. It was once believed that autistic children later developed schizophrenia, but this is not true. Some people with schizophrenia may experience symptoms that resemble those of autism. However, schizophrenics also experience delusions and hallucinations that autistic individuals do not.

Environmental factors are still another area that some claim are linked to autism. In some places where environmental toxins have been identified, there may be a greater incidence of autism. Further investigation is needed to determine whether a valid connection exists between these factors. Various food additives, vaccines, and the overuse of antibiotics have also been blamed for the disorder.

Answers are essential because while its cause remains unknown, autism appears to be on the rise. A recent report to the California state legislature indicated that the number of autistic children in the state's special-education programs increased by 273 percent between 1987 and 1998. That number is considered exceptionally high because other disability categories increased by only about 50 percent. There are those, however, who argue that the seemingly high increase in autism merely reflects better diagnostic techniques. They further stress that all special-education programs are growing due to the public's increased awareness of the available resources.

Nevertheless, former California state senator Rick Rolles, who is the parent of an autistic child, argues that there is an undeniable increase in autism. He noted that places where the incidence of autism is unusually high "are not clusters of autism but snapshots of what is occurring nationwide."[7]

CHAPTER FOUR

Treatment

ALTHOUGH NO CURE for autism exists at this time, help is available for people with this disorder. A number of treatments have vastly improved the quality of life for many autistic individuals. Because autism's symptoms vary tremendously from case to case, no single treatment is beneficial to everyone. Therefore, an individualized treatment plan must be worked out for each patient to help that person advance in specific areas that have been especially difficult for him or her.

In some cases, several types of treatment are combined to yield optimum results. For example, medication may be prescribed to reduce certain undesirable behaviors in an individual, while an educational program might also be helpful in allowing that person to improve his or her skills. As the National Institute of Mental Health states: "Today [an autistic] child who

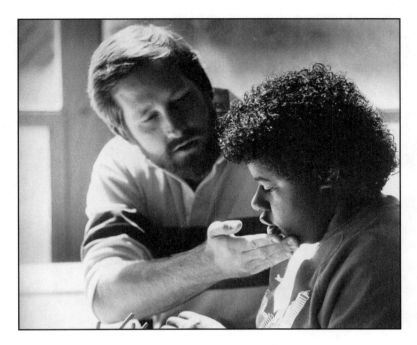

A teacher works with an autistic girl in a public school special education class.

receives effective therapy and education has every hope of using his or her unique capacity to learn. Even some who are seriously mentally retarded can often master many self-help skills such as cooking, dressing, doing laundry, and handling money. For such children, greater independence and self-care may be the primary training goals. Other youngsters may go on to learn basic academic skills, like reading, writing, and simple math. Many complete high school. Some . . . may even earn college degrees. Like anyone else, their personal interests provide strong incentives to learn."[1]

Professionals stress that early intervention is crucial

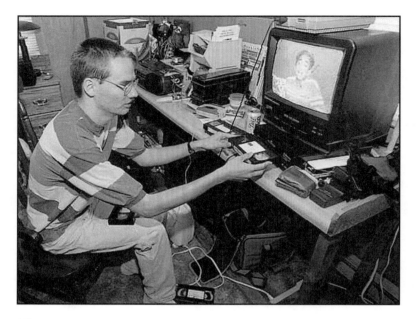

This autistic 19-year-old is a high school graduate and avid film-maker. He is preparing to move into an apartment with his older brother.

for children with autism. Programs especially geared to the child's needs at a young age greatly enhance that person's chances of significantly improving his or her lifelong functioning. Dr. Contance Lalinec, a psychologist at Montreal Children's Hospital in Quebec, Canada, who works with toddlers with developmental delays noted that: "The early years are crucial because the brain is more malleable in young children."

"Language skills are the key to social success later in life," added Dr. Peter Szatmari, a professor of psychiatry at the Centre for the Studies of Children at Risk at McMaster University in Hamilton, Ontario, Canada. "If you can improve the capacity for developing language through early intervention, you really do seem to be able to make a profound impact on their outcome several years later."2

The NIMH provided the following hypothetical case involving a preschool girl named Janie as an example of how early intervention can help: "Today, at age four, Janie is enrolled in an intensive program in which she is trained at home by her mother and several specialists. She is beginning to show real progress. She now makes eye contact and has begun to talk. She can ask for things. As a result, she seems happier, less frustrated, and better able to form connections with others. She's also begun to show some remarkable skills. She can

A kindergarten class at a school for autistic children in Salt Lake City

stack blocks and match objects with a skill far beyond her years. And her memory is amazing. Although her speech is often unclear, she can recite and act out entire television programs. Her parents' dream is that she will progress enough to enter a regular kindergarten next year."[3]

Some of the better-known forms of treatment available for autistic children are discussed below.

EDUCATIONAL/BEHAVIORAL TREATMENTS

These therapies often stress highly structured individualized sessions. Consistency and a predictable schedule of daily activities help autistic young people plan and organize their experiences. The emphasis in such programs is on changing negative behaviors and learning new skills. Sometimes a skill will be broken down into smaller parts so that the individual can grasp and practice each part before going on to the next. Something as seemingly simple as combing one's hair may be broken down into at least 10 smaller steps. Children with severe autism will usually need to be taught in a one-on-one setting, or with just a few other students.

Some autistic students are able to get along in a broader educational arena with some assistance. What the students learn depends on their ability. Those with mild autism may study the traditional subjects taught to all students. Those with more severe cases concentrate on more basic skills. When dealing with higher-functioning autistic young people, the same basic learning techniques are applied to more complex situations.

The NIMH described how this can occur as follows: "Although higher-functioning children may be able to handle academic work, they too need help to organize the task and avoid distractions. A student with autism might be assigned the same addition problems as her classmates. But instead of assigning several pages in the textbook, the teacher might give her one page at a time or make a list of specific tasks to be checked off as each is done."[4]

In getting autistic children the help they need, special attention is often paid to improving communication and social skills. Sometimes, communication aids such as electronic communication devices or picture communication boards prove helpful. In any case, the goal is to develop useful communication skills.

As noted by the National Institute on Deafness and Other Communication Disorders (NIDCD): "For some, verbal communication is a realistic goal. For others, the goal may be gestured communication. Still others may have the goal of communicating by means of a symbol system such as picture boards. Treatment should include periodic in-depth evaluations provided by an individual with special training in the evaluation and treatment of speech and language disorders, such as a speech-language pathologist."[5]

Perhaps the greatest challenge facing any autistic young person is ultimately learning to interact effectively with others in real-life situations. "Children with autism need to be taught how to play and how to act in a social situation," explained Dr. Cathy Pratt, director of the Indiana Resource Center for Autism. "They don't learn by observing, the way most people do. Instead they need to be shown and told what to do. They prefer

A teacher and her autistic student work on matching words with objects.

following a clearly defined set of rules. To help them [in the area of making friends] we explain what questions are OK to ask. We tell them how to behave in the cafeteria or in a classroom, and what kind of things are appropriate to do at recess."[6]

Many behaviorally based intervention programs build on the autistic child's basic strengths and interests. At times speech therapy, music therapy, and occupational therapy are relied on. Physical therapy is useful for autistic children who need to improve their motor skills—coordination, muscle strength, and control. In addition to individual treatment, autistic students can also sometimes benefit from physical-education settings in which they have an opportunity to be with other children in a game or playground atmosphere.

Parents may be trained to give their child special help as well. As the mother of one autistic boy put it— "The bottom line is that raising [my son] was not all that different from raising any other child. Like any youngster, he needed to learn certain rules, and to understand that there are consequences for his actions. It might take a kid like... [my son] longer to grasp a concept, but once he learns it, he learns it for good."[7]

Parent involvement has often been shown to be a major factor in the treatment's success. "Parents work with teachers and therapists to identify the behaviors to be changed and the skills to be taught," the National Institute of Mental Health explained. "Recognizing that parents are the child's earliest teachers, more programs are beginning to train parents to continue therapy at home. Research is beginning to suggest that mothers and fathers who are trained to work with their child can be as effective as professional teachers and therapists."[8]

Families seeking help for an autistic child will usually need both educational and medical assistance. Often their local school system will be a good resource for much of the educational help they'll need. Under a federal law known as the Individuals with Disabilities Education Act (IDEA), students with disabilities (including autism) are entitled to a free and appropriate public education. Educating an autistic student frequently includes providing related services such as behavior modification as well as other types of therapy.

Because autism takes many forms, parents must consider their child's unique needs in finding the treatment options that will be best for that particular individual. The National Institute of Mental Health provides the following checklist of questions as a guide in making these decisions:

- How successful has the program been for other children?

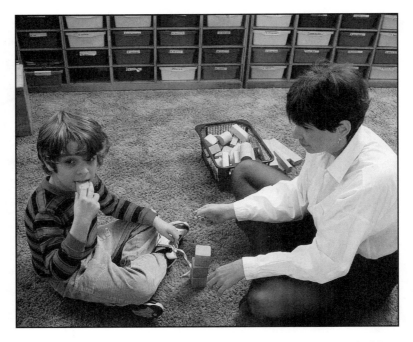

The education of autistic students in public schools is provided by federal law.

- How many children have gone on to placement in a regular school and how have they performed?
- Do staff members have training and experience in working with children and adolescents with autism?
- How are activities planned and organized?
- Are there predictable daily schedules and routines?
- How much individual attention will my child receive?
- How is progress measured? Will my child's behavior be closely observed and recorded?
- Will my child be given tasks and rewards that are personally motivating?
- Is the environment designed to minimize disruptions?
- Will the program prepare me to continue the therapy at home?
- What is the cost, time commitment, and location of the program?[9]

No particular drug will make the varied aspects of autism disappear, but doctors frequently prescribe a variety of medications to lessen some autistic behaviors. Children with autism sometimes develop epilepsy or seizurelike brain activity. Often the seizures appear at about the time young autistic children begin to lose whatever language they've acquired. In other instances, the seizures start in adolescence. In both cases, antiseizure drugs are often beneficial.

Other medications may be used with autistic children who do not experience pain. As the NIMH explained: "Because many children with autism have sensory disturbances and often seem impervious to pain, scientists are also looking for medications that increase or decrease the transmission of physical sensations. Endorphins are natural painkillers produced by the body. But in certain people with autism, the endorphins seem to go too far in suppressing feeling. Scientists are exploring substances that block the effects of endorphins, to see if they can bring the sense of touch to a more normal range. Such drugs may be helpful to children who experience too little sensation. And once they sense pain, such children would be less likely to bite themselves, bang their heads, or hurt themselves in other ways."[10]

Doctors also prescribe drugs for autistic children to reduce anxiety, hyperactivity, and attention disorders. Usually medications administered to quiet autistic symptoms are most effective when used in conjunction with other forms of treatment such as behavior modification or various training programs.

Many of the drugs used to treat autism adjust serotonin levels or affect other brain-signaling chemicals. Dr. Robert DeLong, a pediatric neurologist at Duke University Medical Center in Durham, North Carolina, has done extensive research on the effects of the antidepressant Prozac on autistic children. Apparently some autistic symptoms mirror those of depression. In one study, Dr. DeLong reported that about 20 percent of the patients had a "wonderful response" while another 35 percent showed "a very good response." Approximately 40 percent of those involved in the research showed no response. In evaluating the study's results, DeLong stated: "There's no doubt that serotonin is central to what's happening in autism."[11]

The usefulness of any particular drug in reducing autistic symptoms varies among individuals. In addition, some drugs have severe side effects and these must be weighed against the benefits a patient derives from them. When dealing with young children, it is especially important that the use of all medications be closely monitored.

While the more standard treatments for autism are supported by a substantial amount of research, other treatment avenues are also available. Through the years, various interventions have been touted as "miracle cures" for autism, only to fall by the wayside later on. As the National Institute of Neurological Disorders and Stroke warns: "These therapies remain controversial and may or may not reduce a specific person's symptoms. Parents should use caution before subscribing to any particular treatment."[12]

Research is being done to see if vitamin B_6, taken with magnesium, can stimulate brain activity in autistic children, but as yet no solid scientific evidence suggests that vitamins have any effect on an autistic person's thinking or behavior. Nevertheless, some parents claim that their children have substantially improved after taking megadoses—extremely large amounts—of vitamin B, vitamin C, and a number of different minerals. Similarly, diet supposedly has no effect on autistic behaviors. Yet there are some parents who swear that their autistic youngsters either have a low tolerance for wheat and grain products or are allergic to them. They stress that many of their children's symptoms are dramatically reduced when these foods are excluded.

The diet drug fenfluramine has also been used experimentally with autistic children. Originally designed to help obese adults curb their appetites, the medication supposedly lessened undesirable behaviors in autistic children as well as boosting their ability to concentrate. Although some research indicates that the drug has had a beneficial effect on some young people, other studies showed no significant change.

Perhaps the most recent exciting, if unproven, therapy for autism came in the form of an intestinal hormone known as secretin. At first all the hoopla had centered around a little boy named Parker Beck. His parents, Victoria and Gary Beck, had always wanted a happy healthy family and after their second child Parker was born that seemed to be what they finally had. "We had for a long time envisioned that moment when we'd have a couple of little kids in the back seat of our car and take family trips and do family things and everything had seemed to just fall in step with what we had dreamed about," recalled Victoria Beck.[13]

However, shortly after Parker turned two, a painful reality came crashing down on the family. Their little boy had begun to change and his parents were upset by what they saw. The once cheerful, affectionate child obviously was no longer his old self. "He would not look at us. He would shift his gaze," his mother said in describing the boy's behavior. "He was irritable. He would throw his head back in screams—high-pitched screams."[14]

Parker appeared to be shutting his parents out. He had started speaking but now he stopped. He rarely slept through the night anymore. At first his pediatrician did not seem concerned and assured the Becks that their son would outgrow these changes. But that didn't happen. Instead, Parker's symptoms worsened. After seeing numerous specialists, his parents were faced with a diagnosis they did not want to hear—Parker was autistic. The Becks were determined to return Parker to what he had once been, but their doctor offered little encouragement. He had told the child's mother: "Mrs. Beck, just let me tell you something. Miracles don't happen in these situations. So why don't you stop wasting your time trying to find one."[15]

The Becks even had the unfortunate experience of running into a psychologist who thought Parker's mother might be at the root of her son's problems. As she recalled the experience, "He [the psychologist] sat down with me and said 'Victoria, we have to figure out who we are treating here, you or Parker.' And I said, 'I don't care who you think you're treating, I'm telling you there's something wrong with my son, and either you jump on board and help me, or I'll go out this door right now and I'll walk down the street, [and] keep walking until I find a doctor who will.' "[16]

Besides Parker's unusual behavior, he had also developed some serious health problems. The little boy now had continual diarrhea and frequent vomiting. There seemed to be nothing anyone could do for him so, after nearly two years, his parents brought him to the University of Maryland medical system to see if someone there could find the key to their son's digestive problems. Parker was given a test called an endoscopy to enable the doctors to pinpoint any digestive irregularities. Unfortunately, the test yielded no definite answers and the Becks felt as if they were again facing a stone wall.

But then—only days later—things began to change. Parker's diarrhea stopped and he slept through the night. But something even more remarkable happened—he started talking and interacting with those around him. Victoria Beck described the first time she heard him talk this way: "Ten days after the procedure, Parker's therapist called me downstairs and said, 'I think you better come here and take a look at this.' And Parker, who had been totally nonverbal was now responding to flash cards as quickly as the therapist could hold them up. She was holding up a picture of me and he was saying, 'Mommy.' And then she held up Gary's picture, and he said, 'Daddy.' We were stunned."[17]

The only change had been the test the boy underwent at the University of Maryland hospital. The Becks felt certain that the answer to his recovery lay there. "We asked the hospital to tell us exactly what he was given," Victoria Beck explained. "Give us the dosage of your anesthesia," she had insisted. "Tell us exactly what you do in the procedure."[18] After analyzing every detail of their son's experience, the Becks realized that Parker had received a small amount of a hormone called secretin. They told the doctors that they thought the drug had inadvertently brought about this remarkable improvement in their son's condition but soon saw that the medical community was not about to be convinced.

To add to the Becks' anxiety, after giving Parker another dose of the hormone, the doctors refused to continue administering it to the boy. Secretin had never been approved by the Federal Drug Administration

(FDA) as a treatment for autism—or any other disorder. Its only approved use was as an aid in diagnosing digestive problems and that was the reason Parker had received it to begin with.

Although doctors are legally permitted to prescribe a drug for a use other than the one for which it was intended and FDA-approved, many hesitate to do so. And that attitude was what Parker's mother ran into as she tried to find a doctor to prescribe secretin for her son. Months passed without Parker getting any more of what his parents had come to consider a miracle drug. Fortunately, the boy did not slip back into his former state but there was no further improvement and his parents did not know what to expect if they weren't able to secure the drug for their son. After an exhaustive search, the Becks finally found a physician who agreed to help them. He prescribed secretin for Parker and once again the boy seemed to be making progress.

As the parents of other autistic children heard about the Becks' success, some dared to hope that secretin might work for their children as well. No one was quite sure what the drug did, but there are those who believe that regulating digestive problems in autistic children may bring about vital changes in their brain chemistry. This was just speculation, however, no one knew for certain whether Parker Beck's improvement was a fluke or if secretin would bring about similar changes in most autistic young people.

Anxious to alleviate their children's symptoms, numerous parents sought out physicians to prescribe the drug. Because of the overwhelming demand, Ferring Pharmaceuticals, the drug company that first manufactured secretin, temporarily ran out of it. That meant desperate parents now had to pay $200 to $1,000 for the scarce vials of secretin. There were other problems as well. Many doctors persisted in their refusal to use the drug without the benefit of FDA testing and approval.

Among these was Dr. Robert Mahourail, a pediatric specialist, who argued—"No one knows what it [secretin] does to the brain. Before we start using it, we should study it. We want to make sure we don't hurt kids."[19] Critical of the fact that the Becks had told their story on the television show *Dateline*, pediatric-neurologist Dr. Robert DeLong echoed Mahourail's concerns when he stated: "The way to do medical research is not to put it on *Dateline* when you have one case and get everybody excited. My feeling is that we've seen a number of these flash-in-the-pan therapies that become famous . . . and it turns out not to amount to anything."[20]

Not all physicians felt this way though. Dr. Paul Hardy of Hingham, Massachusetts, has specialized in treating autistic children for more than 20 years. Prior to the Becks' success with secretin, Hardy had heard a presentation indicating that quite a few autistic children suffered from an overgrowth of yeast in their intestinal tracts. He began to investigate this possibility in his own patients noting, "I was just blown away because of the frequency of gastrointestinal problems in this population."[21]

Hardy had tried secretin on a patient with dramatic results. In under a week, the child was beginning to talk as well as make eye contact. Since that time, Hardy has given the drug to other patients and reports that 30 to 50 percent of these children have improved.

The wonderful success stories include that of four-year-old Caleb, an autistic child who had not spoken since he was two. Caleb had another trait in common with Parker Beck—he did not sleep through the night. Instead of using his bed, the child would lie on the floor on his stomach. When he woke during the night, he'd often forcefully bang his head on the floor, sometimes causing the dishes to rattle in the kitchen cabinets below.

Sometimes the head banging resulted in nosebleeds and bloody lips. Caleb's parents did what they could to comfort and care for him but it was difficult to adequately meet their child's needs. "He can't communicate what's wrong," his mother explained. "He can bang his head for five hours straight."[22]

Caleb often smiled but, like many autistic children, he would not hug his parents or sit on their laps. At times he threw things and when passing an end table would usually knock everything off it to clear the surface. Exasperated, his mother eventually emptied the room of knickknacks.

To everyone's relief, things finally changed soon after Caleb was given secretin. One day as his father watched TV the boy climbed onto his lap and hugged him. At about the same time, Caleb could be spotted feeding himself yogurt with a plastic spoon. His parents agreed that previously their son probably would have tossed the spoon across the room. That evening, Caleb tugged at his mother's T-shirt to draw her closer to him. He hugged and kissed her and when she tickled him, he giggled. "This is worth anything," his mother said. "It's been just phenomenal, like a miracle. He's telling us what he wants. Everything doesn't have to be trial and error."[23]

There have been other success stories as well. Five-year-old Tom also made substantial gains after taking secretin. "He's doing wonderful," the boy's mother reported to a physician. "His appetite is incredible. He's eating pancakes. Before, we were force-feeding him. Now he's eating everything he can get his hands on."[24]

These moving success stories inspired thousands of parents of autistic children throughout America, creating a rush for the drug that soon resulted in chronic shortages. Parents who wanted secretin for their children often spent hours on the Internet hoping to find supplies of the drug that might be shipped here from abroad, as well as local doctors to prescribe it. In many cases parents, rather than medical personnel, were directing the course of their children's treatment and with an untested drug involved, some felt there might be cause for concern.

The dangers were real. Before long, people began to hear tales about secretin that were not as glowing. One unsettling account came from the mother of a nine-year-old autistic boy named Joseph. She had located a doctor to prescribe secretin for her son but the results were devastating. Joseph's condition quickly deteriorated. The boy showed no interest in eating and he stopped saying the few words that made up his vocabulary. "He was biting, hitting, and kicking after the secretin," his mother related. "I wish I knew then what I know now. I want parents to know that negatives can happen. Every time you see secretin on TV they never tell you that something bad can happen."[25]

Marie Bristol-Power, program director for autism and related disorders at the National Institute of Child Health and Human Development has warned parents to be wary of claims they hear about miracle cures. "There's an awful lot of information and misinformation on the Internet, so it doesn't take you very long to think that you know all you need to know. [But] some of what's on the Internet is not accurate. . . . For a significant number of children there are negative side effects [with secretin]—exaggerated excitability, aggressiveness, hyperactivity, and irritability. For many it's transient [temporary] but for others there are long-term effects."[26] In addition, no one can be sure of how long a single dose will last. Some say from five to six weeks but of course that might vary depending on the amount given.

Bristol-Power has further noted that 40 percent of the drug secretin is made up of other chemicals introduced during the manufacturing process. This raises the question of whether the benefits or side effects experienced by the children are actually coming from the secretin or from something it is combined with. Safety, regarding the ongoing use of secretin, is another concern that's frequently expressed. So far, secretin has only been FDA-approved for gastrointestinal testing at a single low-dose level. It is still not known whether repeated large doses of the medication will produce other side effects over time.

Some scientists have further suggested that as secretin comes from pigs, it could create a dangerous bridge through which animal diseases might be transmitted to humans. "When insulin was first made, it was a pig product," recalled Jill Belchic, a psychologist at Children's Seashore House. "After repeated doses, some children stopped responding and others had a shock reaction. I am recommending that parents should participate in . . . controlled studies to determine safe and effective doses and help us identify kids who can respond from kids who won't."[27]

Of course, testing takes time—especially studies that follow large numbers of children over a period of years to determine the long-term effects of a drug. Among the earliest short-term secretin studies was the work conducted at the Olson Huff Center for Child Development at the Thomas Rehabilitation Hospital in Asheville, North Carolina. The study involved 56 children—half of whom were given secretin while the other half received a placebo (a substance that does nothing). Neither the children participating nor their parents knew who was getting the drug, and who was taking the placebo.

The results reported in *The New England Journal of Medicine* in December 1999 revealed that the children receiving the secretin had shown no significant improvement. Yet even the scientists conducting the study admitted that the research had its shortcomings. Those involved noted, "Our study had its weaknesses. First, this was a short-term study, and it is unlikely that significant changes can occur in a brain-based disorder within days or weeks. Second, this was a single-dose study and multiple doses may prove to be efficacious [helpful] . . ."[28] Other problems involved the accuracy of the diagnostic instruments used.

Much more research is needed. Interestingly, after being told that the single dose of secretin had not benefited their children, 69 percent of the parents of study participants indicated that they nevertheless wanted more secretin for their children. Obviously, they thought there might be benefits from further treatment.

As Bernard Rimland, Director of the Autism Research Institute and the father of an autistic son put it, "This [study] is the top of the first inning. There is a tremendous backlog of very convincing, very hard-to-explain-away case-history data showing, in many kids, a remarkable response that simply does not occur under normal circumstances. . . . Immediately after getting secretin, kids who never had a bowel movement have a normal bowel movement. Kids who never slept the night through, sleep the night through. Kids who never said 'Daddy' are beginning to react to their parents."[29]

Since then a number of other small studies have

Dolphin therapy for autistic children.

been reported. There are signs that some autistic children with gastrointestinal problems may respond well to secretin. However, this has not been conclusively shown. The only thing that is certain is that more research is needed.

Will secretin eventually prove to be a valuable piece in the puzzle autism presents? In the future, scientists are likely to learn whether or not it really works. If it does, there may eventually be an effective synthetic form of the drug that eliminates any impurities derived from the pig product. However, the importance of scientific study prior to the use of any costly and potentially harmful treatment cannot be underestimated. In this instance and others like it, only time and further study can provide the vital answers needed.

CHAPTER FIVE

Strides

PEOPLE THINK OF autism as a children's disease, but these children grow up and there's still no cure. The well-known neurologist Oliver Sacks acknowledged this phenomenon when he wrote of autistic individuals: "Indeed, in a strange way, most people speak only of autistic children and never of autistic adults, as if the children somehow just vanished from the earth."[1] When autistic individuals turn 21, many of the government-mandated educational programs and services for them end. As Christopher McDoyle, who started a clinic for adults with autism warned—"A person with autism can be sent to an institution or even a nursing home for the rest of his life."[2]

Neurologist Dr. Oliver Sacks

Fortunately, things have started to change in recent years. In many cases, enhanced training programs have provided autistic individuals with vital independent living skills and some symptoms of the disorder have improved through proper medication. Anne McBride of Cornell University Medical Center summed up the current state of affairs when she said, "We're much more aware now that autism is a complex, heterogeneous, lifelong condition and that many of the behavioral problems that interfere with functioning are amenable with [can be helped by] medication." She went on to say that even if undesirable behaviors are only reduced by 50 percent, for some adults with autism "this can mean the difference between not functioning and being capable of living in a sheltered or mainstream environment."[3]

About 5 to 10 percent of autistic adults are capable of leading fully independent lives. Another 25 percent improve with age, but still need to live in a supervised setting. In New York City, for example, some such autistic individuals reside together in a group home, supporting themselves by making items that are sold in a retail store. A woman named Anita Zatlow, who has an autistic son, started the shop. "Our approach is practical," she said in describing the endeavor. "They work, earn money, and participate in the community to the best of their abilities."[4]

Autistic teens can prepare for a more independent adult life at places like Hyman House in Huntington, West Virginia. Operated through the Autism Services Center, this group home is staffed 24 hours a day by adults who assist the residents and keep track of their progress. To help the residents master simple skills,

Residents of a group home for autistic adults. The man in front is using a Wolf board to ask for more food.

tasks are broken down into small steps and the teen residents are evaluated on each step before progressing to the next.

Some have made remarkable progress. These autistic teens either attend public school or work with teachers at Hyman House. They learn to make their beds, do their laundry, and help with other household chores. In some cases, these are skills their families never expected them to achieve. "I think the Lord answered our prayers," the father of one of the boys at Hyman House said. "I don't think our son will ever be normal, but he has . . . gone further than my highest expectations."[5]

The NIMH cites the following hypothetical case as typical of a young autistic individual who has successfully achieved a degree of independence: "Adolescence was a good time for Paul. He seemed to relax and become more social. He became more affectionate. When approached, he would converse with people. For several months, drugs were used to help him control his aggression, but they were stopped because they caused unwanted side effects. Even so, he now rarely throws or breaks things.

"Two years ago, Paul's parents were able to take advantage of new scientific understanding about autism, and they enrolled him in an innovative program that provides full-time support, enabling him to live and work in the community. Today, at 20, he has a closely supervised job assembling booklets for a publishing company. He lives in an attractive apartment with another man who has autism, and a residence supervisor. Paul loves picnics and outings to the library to check out books and cassettes. He also enjoys going home each week to visit his family. But he still demands familiarity and order. As soon as he arrives home, he moves every piece of furniture back to the location that is familiar to him."[6]

Today, programs throughout the country are changing the lives of autistic people. Through individualized placement programs, increasing numbers of autistic adults in the Rockville, Maryland, area take buses to 14 work sites. "People laughed at us," recalled Doreen Coleman, Director of the Vocational Program at

Community Services for Autistic Adults and Children, "when we told them three years ago what we intended for autistic adults in our community."[7] But they didn't laugh for long. The autistic adults in the program work in production jobs assembling small parts, fastening parts together, and doing other such tasks. Often their employers find that they complete these jobs faster and with more accuracy than other employees.

One plant manager described Don's (an autistic staff member) performance as follows: "This is the job I had when I started working here. I remember how tedious it was, how I would, as I worked on the copper tubing, invent little games to play with the materials and new ways to vary the routine. But Don doesn't find it boring and his attention doesn't wander. He works steadily and gets the job done."[8] A supervisor at another job site added—"[This work needs to be done but] most people just can't take it very long. They want to move on to something different, more sophisticated. I have even had construction workers, out of work because of a physical disability, try this job, but they quit."[9]

The vocational counselors placing the autistic workers realized that these individuals might be uniquely valuable to small manufacturing firms. "We didn't tell employers that we wanted them to be do-gooders and hire the handicapped," asserted Director of Community Services Patricia Juhrs. "In fact, we didn't talk much about disability or autism. Instead we told them we had workers who could perform simple mechanical tasks effectively and would want to stay on the job. In addition, our program would provide the job training and place a full-time job-site counselor to maintain the training and to take care of any problems related to the disability."[10]

These job counselors remain near the workers, helping them to keep focused on the task at hand as well as adjust to any changes in the schedule or routine. They also assist the workers in learning to use public transportation. The NIMH describes the role such community-based counselors play in helping autistic people at the workplace this way: "Job and residence coaches, who serve as a link between the program participants and the community, are the key to such programs. As few as two adults with autism may be assigned to each coach. The job coach demonstrates the steps of a job to the worker, observes behavior, and regularly acknowledges good performance. The job coach also serves as a bridge between workers with autism and their co-workers. For example, the coach steps in if a worker loses self-control or presents any problems on the job. The coach also provides training in specific social skills, such as waving or saying hello to fellow workers. At home, the residence coach reinforces social and self-help behaviors, and finds ways to help people manage their time and responsibilities."[11]

After two of the autistic workers in the Rockville, Maryland, program had been with a firm for more than three years, the corporate newsletter published a story on them that perhaps best sums up the overall effect of this community-based effort. The article stated: "Mary (Saverbrier) was spending her days sitting alone in a locked room at the state hospital before Community Services counselors decided to see what could be done for her. Bill (Novotny) was withdrawn and seldom spoke. Today, both are welcome and productive workers sitting alongside other productive employees. Each has mastered a variety of skills and has proven to be a conscientious, steady, and much admired member of the [company]."12

The NIMH cites that presently "about a third of all people with autism can live and work in the community with some degree of independence." They expect that "as scientific research points the way to more effective

An autistic man boxes batteries at a warehouse. Austistic people are often suited to repetitive work.

therapies and as communities establish programs that provide proper support" these numbers will increase.[13]

Some very high-functioning autistic individuals live entirely on their own and may attend college and become professionals. Often these individuals are said to have Asperger's Syndrome. There has been some debate over whether Asperger's Syndrome is truly a separate disorder from autism. However, neurologist Oliver Sacks described the difference between people with Asperger's Syndrome and those with autism this way: "The ultimate difference, perhaps, is this: people with Asperger's Syndrome can tell us of their experiences, their inner feelings and states, whereas those with classical autism cannot. With classical autism, there is no window, and we can only infer. With Asperger's Syndrome, there is self-consciousness and at least some power to introspect and report."[14]

Perhaps the best-known high-functioning autistic individual is a woman named Temple Grandin who has a Ph.D. in Animal Science from the University of Illinois. A proven leader in her field, Dr. Grandin won an award in 1995 for redesigning livestock equipment to lessen the panic or pain animals may experience when slaughtered. Today, Temple Grandin is an assistant professor in the Animal Sciences Department at Colorado State University as well as a consultant on livestock behavior and facility design. But as a child, her future hadn't looked as bright.

Grandin was extremely sensitive to sounds and smells and lived in a world of exaggerated sensations. She experienced even mild noises as though they were at an overwhelming volume. Her family also had to deal with her persistent behavior problems. She describes what her childhood was like below:

"Normal children use clay for modeling; I used my feces and then spread my creations all over the room. I chewed up puzzles and spit the cardboard mush out on the floor. I had a violent temper, and when thwarted, I'd throw anything handy—a museum-quality vase or leftover feces. I screamed continually."[15]

Other classic autism symptoms also characterized her daily existence: "Spinning was another favorite activity," she recalled. "I'd sit on the floor and twirl around. The room spun with me. This self-stimulatory behavior made me feel powerful, in control of things. After all, I could make a whole room turn around. Sometimes I made the whole world spin by twisting the swing in our backyard so that the chains would wind up. Then I'd sit there as the swing unwound, watching the sky and earth whirl. I realize that nonautistic children enjoy twirling around in a swing too. The difference is that the autistic child is obsessed with the act of spinning."[16]

The symptoms of the disorder set Temple Grandin apart from other children her age. The occasions that they eagerly looked forward to were often hideous for her. Describing how she felt, Grandin noted, "Like birthday parties. They were torture for me. The confusion created by noisemakers suddenly going off startled me. I would invariably react by hitting another child or by picking up an ashtray or anything else that was handy and flinging it across the room. . . . Even today, sudden loud noises such as a motorcycle's sound, are still painful to me."[17]

The holiday season, filled with special dinners, parties, and guests was a powerful assault on the young girl's senses as well. "Ordinary days with a change in schedule or unexpected events threw me into a frenzy, but Thanksgiving or Christmas was even worse. At those times, our home bulged with relatives. The clamor of many voices, the different smells—perfume, cigars, damp wool caps or gloves—people moving about at different speeds, going in different directions, the constant noise and confusion, the constant touching, were overwhelming. One very, very overweight aunt, who was generous and caring, let me use her professional oil paints. I like her. Still, when she hugged me, I was totally engulfed and I panicked. It was like being suffocated by a mountain of marshmallows. I withdrew because her abundant affection overwhelmed my nervous system."[18]

To balance that part of her, however, Temple Grandin also had tremendous powers of concentration that could bring a sense of quiet and order to a world that often seemed harrowing to her. She wrote, "I could sit on the beach for hours dribbling sand through my fingers and fashioning miniature mountains. Each particle of sand intrigued me as though I were a scientist looking through a microscope. Other times I scrutinized each line in my finger, following each one as if it were a road on a map."[19]

When she was three, Grandin had been taken to a neurologist who diagnosed her as autistic. Particularly upset by the young girl's complete lack of language, the doctor warned her parents that Temple might have to be institutionalized. Fortunately, that never happened.

If it had, Grandin feels she would have been on the other end of the spectrum as a poorly functioning autistic individual. Instead she was helped by an excellent early preschool and teachers who worked hard to build on her strengths to help her reach her full potential.

In addition to her present university teaching position, Temple Grandin has her own company and does consulting on livestock facility design in countries around the globe. She feels a special bond to animals, which may account for some of the success she's had in devising effective management systems for them. "Cattle are disturbed by the same sort of sounds as autistic people," Grandin explained, "high pitched sounds, air hissing, or sudden loud noises; they cannot adapt to these. But they are not bothered by low-pitched, rumbling noises. They are disturbed by high visual contrasts, shadows or sudden movements. A light touch will make them pull away, a firm touch calms them. The way I would pull away from being touched is the way a wild cow will pull away—getting me used to being touched is very similar to taming a wild cow."[20]

Temple Grandin has been remarkably successful in the work world. She has done exceedingly well for someone with—or without—autism. Grandin has published more than 300 papers on her work in animal management and her insights into her disorder. Nevertheless, she admits that in some ways, autism has left her at a loss in social situations. She has remarked that while she's able to comprehend "simple, strong universal emotions," she's at a loss when it comes to more subtle cues or the manipulative game-playing people often engage in. In this area, she remains an observer, still very much on the outside looking in. As she describes it, "Much of the time, I feel like an anthropologist on Mars."[21]

"My work is my life," she confessed. "There's not much else." In an article she wrote, Grandin further described her social activities, stating:

"I do not fit in with the social life of my town or university. Almost all of my social contacts are with livestock people or people interested in autism. Most of my Friday and Saturday nights are spent writing papers and drawings. My interests are factual and my recreational reading consists mostly of science and livestock publications. I have little interest in novels with complicated interpersonal relationships, because I am unable to remember the sequence of events. Detailed descriptions of new technologies in science fiction or descriptions of exotic places are much more interesting. My life would be horrible if I did not have my challenging career."[22]

It should be noted that, with time and practice, Temple Grandin overcame still more of the barriers that separate autistic people from others in society. Initially, when Grandin lectured on either autism or animal science, she never made eye contact with the audience or took questions from the floor. Now she is able to do both. In recent years, she has also started spending time with two or three people she's become somewhat close to. That is a difficult but important accomplishment for any autistic person. It is also a valued step forward for a woman who as a schoolgirl had always wanted to have friends, but could not help acting in a way that often alienated others. "I couldn't figure out what I was doing wrong," she said of her experience. "I had an odd

lack of awareness that I was different. I could never figure out why I didn't fit in."[23]

Despite the difficulties it has sometimes presented,
Grandin does not regret the person she has become and
the role autism has played in her development. She
once ended a lecture by saying, "If I could snap my fingers and not be autistic, I would not—because then I
wouldn't be me."[24] Though aware that she has missed
out on some things because of autism, she still feels that
there's value in the way autistic people perceive the
world. In 1990, Grandin wrote, "Aware adults with
autism and their parents are often angry about autism.
They may ask why God or nature created such horrible
conditions as autism, manic depression, and schizophrenia. However, if the genes that caused these conditions were eliminated, there might be a terrible price to
pay. It is possible that persons with bits of these traits
are more creative or possibly even geniuses. . . . If science eliminated these genes, maybe the whole world
would be taken over by accountants."[25]

Contributing what she can to society is extremely
important to Temple Grandin. As she told neurologist
Oliver Sacks, "I'd like to hope that if there's no personal
afterlife, some energy or impression is left on the uni-
verse. . . . Most people can pass on genes—I can pass
on thoughts or what I write. I've read that libraries are
where immortality lies. . . . I don't want my thoughts to
die with me. . . . I want to leave something. . . . I'm not
interested in power, or piles of money. I want to leave
something behind. I want to make a powerful contribu-
tion—know that my life has meaning. Right now, I'm
talking about things at the core of my existence."[26]

While Temple Grandin is extremely well known for

her achievements, there are other autistic people who, like her, have done quite well professionally. Many high-functioning individuals with the disorder have made significant strides in the computer field. "There is something about computers that is very autism-friendly," noted Ami Klin, assistant professor of child psychology at Yale University Medical School. "Computers are very rigid, and so are the people we work with. One of my clients once had a very nice insight," Klin added. "He described himself as a computer simulation of a human being. He tried to decode the social world in a way that a computer would try to make sense of it."27

As might be expected, Temple Grandin feels very much at home with computers and has sometimes used them as a way to help explain how her mind operates. "All of my memories are stored as images," she has said. "I can go and look at these pictures like Web pages on the Internet. I can run the equipment [I design] in my head the way you would on a 3-D graphics workstation. I used to think everybody could do that. Programming is a good profession for autistic people," she added, "because they can sit at a terminal and turn out beautiful work, and no one cares how weird they are. They are visual thinkers, so they will tend to go for the graphics stuff."28

Sara R. S. Miller, president of Nova Systems, Inc., in Milwaukee, is autistic but has done well professionally in information systems. Miller's thinking enables her to immediately detect errors in software by identifying flaws in coding patterns. "I have a very limited black-and-white interpretation of the world," Miller remarked. "And in computer programming, you either have the bit on or off; there are no half bits. . . . When I do my coding, it just flies because I can keep so much in my brain at once," Miller continued. "I can get stuff done in five or six hours that would take others two days to do."[29]

Autistic individuals often do best in workplaces that are quiet and predictable and where a project's goals are clearly defined. "I can't work in a noisy environment," Sara Miller commented, "but I can fixate so much on the work, I get two to three times as much work done."[30] Like many others in her position, Miller learned to build on her strengths to overcome the disadvantages associated with autism. However, she admits that some work situations set her on edge. For example, an autistic person's lack of social skills often makes it difficult to meet new clients or participate in office interactions. "It's like I'm always running a video camera," Miller explained. "I can't think my way out of a brown paper bag if I haven't seen something before. . . . To see a new customer on my own would make me freeze. It's this overwhelming fear that a lion, tiger, or bear is going to jump out at me. So my business partner and I go for the first time together. On the next call I can go myself. I've built a visual memory of where all the parts and pieces are, and I know where to look for the lions, tigers, and bears."[31]

As computers increasingly become more a part of everyday life, high-functioning autistic individuals may be able to forge a greater role for themselves in various professional arenas. "I've been obsessed with computers since I was 11," noted Martijn Dekker, a young autistic man from the Netherlands who runs a support group for autistic people on the Internet. "Groups, such as mine, seem to do away with the myth that autistics do not want to make contact with other human beings," Dekker stressed. "Given the means that work for us—a computer, an Internet connection, and a small virtual community of neurologically similar souls—we are able to form very deep and meaningful contacts."[32]

CHAPTER SIX
Savants

We've seen that some people with autism learn to function extremely well. But besides those who participate quite effectively in society, about 10 percent of autistic people appear to possess some truly extraordinary abilities. These individuals are known as "savants." Often their skills lie in the areas of music, math, or drawing. Some savants can memorize train schedules or pages out of a telephone book. They may do calendar calculations that amaze us—citing the day of the week on which an event occurred several years ago. These skills exist despite the person's inability to get along in most other ways, as is evident in the following case study:

"One seven-year-old autistic child was a true musical genius. He could play many instruments and on hearing a melody could instantly reproduce it on any of his instruments. He could also immediately transpose the tune into any key desired and compose appropriate harmonies. While few would doubt that this child had musical talent, the usefulness of his skills was questionable; he was neither toilet trained, nor able to say his name, nor to respond to a simple command such as 'close the door.' "[1]

Both researchers and the public have been fascinated by the savant's skills through the years. One well-known autistic savant was a six-year-old English girl named Nadia. In 1973, Nadia's mother had taken her to the University of Nottingham Child Development Research Unit in Nottingham, England. The previous year Nadia had been diagnosed as displaying "autistic behavior and possible considerable psychiatric disturbance," and unfortunately it was obvious that the diagnosis was on target.[2]

Nadia displayed many of the classic symptoms of the disorder. She avoided eye contact and insisted on a high degree of consistency or sameness in her surroundings. Nadia did not socialize and her language skills were extremely limited. At times, she would withdraw into herself and stare out into space or simply wander aimlessly about the room.

In many ways, Nadia was very much like many of the autistic children seen at the hospital. However, there was one big difference. This little girl was an exceptional artist. Members of the hospital staff who had analyzed and judged over 24,000 pictures done by British children for a contest were convinced that Nadia's work was far superior to any of the others.

Several things about Nadia's drawings made her

artwork especially remarkable. In many cases, her drawings were copies of pictures she had seen only once. The child drew quickly and methodically—often creating a number of segmented lines that she later joined to form her subject. Though in many ways, Nadia might have been considered a somewhat gawky or awkward child, when holding a pencil her hand became a graceful instrument that seemed to glide across the paper.

Nadia especially liked to draw horses, but she also drew other animals and people. Looking at Nadia's work, you might say that the little girl had developed a style all her own. She often used variations of size and shading to make her creations look more alive. Neurologist Oliver Sacks described how Nadia's art was received as follows:

"Her drawings they [the psychologists working with her] felt were different from those of other children: she had a sense of space, an ability to depict appearances and shadows, a sense of perspective such as the most gifted normal child might only develop at three times her age. She constantly experimented with different angles and perspectives. Whereas normal children go through a developmental sequence from random scribbling to schematic and geometric figures to 'tadpole' figures, Nadia seemed to bypass these and move at once into highly recognizable detailed representational drawings."[3]

The hospital therapists working with Nadia thought the child's exceptional artistic ability might have developed to compensate for her lack of language. They believed that in the absence of speech, it was likely that Nadia's artistic talent had blossomed even more. At the time it was thought that these abilities developed at about the same time. Had one flowered because the other never took root?

Nadia's therapists wondered what the effect on her artwork would be if she learned to talk. Lorna Selfe, a psychologist who worked closely with the girl thought her patient's drawing ability might then either greatly diminish or even disappear altogether. Apparently, that's just what happened. At age seven, Nadia entered a school for autistic children where through an intensive effort, her language skills improved. Her flair for drawing, however, disappeared. Once Nadia acquired language, she tended not to show any interest in art. When asked to draw, the caliber of her work was no longer what it had formerly been. Whether her skill had somehow been transferred from one part of the brain to another—or had simply disappeared—remained an unanswered question. Lorna Selfe later wrote a book about Nadia that describes the effect of the trade-off as follows:

"Is this a tragedy? For us who love to be astonished [by amazing savant abilities], maybe. For Nadia, perhaps it is enough to have been a marvelous child. If the partial loss of her gift is the price that must be paid for language—even just enough language to bring her into some kind of community of discourse with her small protected world—we must I think, be prepared to pay that price on Nadia's behalf."[4]

Of course it has never been conclusively proven that acquiring language truly cost Nadia her artistic skill. Other artistic savants have achieved some degree of speech and still retained their special abilities. At times, these special talents have also dissipated following the death of a loved one. It may be significant that just as Nadia entered school, her mother died. Then again, it is also possible that Nadia's loss of skill had nothing to do with either of these circumstances.

Richard Wawro is a savant who retained his exceptional artistic ability despite the considerable therapeutic advances he achieved through the years. As a toddler, Wawro had been diagnosed as both retarded and demonstrating autistic behaviors. Like many autistic individuals, he would withdraw, and he displayed a need for repetition and consistency in his environment. At times, he had violent temper tantrums, while on other days he was content to just repeatedly strike a single key on the piano for hours. Richard, who was fascinated by spinning objects, also loved to twirl about.

Though now a legally blind adult (he has limited vision), Richard had several surgeries for cataracts on both eyes as a boy. The child's artistic promise was first noticed when, at the age of three, he was given a box of chalk. He immediately began filling up the chalkboard in a neighbor's home. Those around him suspected that the boy might have talent but they didn't realize the extent of his ability at first.

At six years of age, Richard Wawro entered a school for special-needs children in Edinburgh, Scotland. There, he was given crayons to use and his ability seemed to blossom. Richard worked quickly and seemingly effortlessly. He used the crayons to create a vast array of pictures in various sizes. At times, he layered the crayoned colors to create a special texture or shading. Molly Leishman, one of Richard's teachers at the school, noticed that he was fascinated by the way flickering light seemed to dance off the surfaces. She made mobiles and toys for the boy out of shiny silver paper that glistened in the sun. Fortunately, it was the breakthrough she had hoped for and Richard responded well. It has since been noted that elements of light and shading are inherent in the richness of Richard's art. Being quite near-sighted, Richard was a child-artist who held the paper close to his face as he worked. Yet the results were fabulous from any angle. By the time Richard turned 12, his work was cited by experts as an "incredible phenomenon rendered with the precision of a mechanic and the vision of a poet."[5] Like his artwork, Richard's memory is remarkable. He can remember where and when he created each of the pictures in his now vast collection. His memory is also crucial to his art as he does not use models but draws from images he has previously seen. Richard, however, does not create exact replicas of these—instead he alters them where necessary to add his own special touch or vision to the final product.

Richard Wawro's talent has brought him international fame and recognition. When he was still a teenager he had his first exhibition at the DeMarco Gallery in Edinburgh, Scotland. That was just the start of his success. Since that time, he has had many more exhibitions and sold more than 1,000 pieces of his work. Former British Prime Minister Margaret Thatcher has cited Richard as being among her favorite artists and Pope John Paul II also owns several of Wawro's works. Some of Richard's pictures have sold for more than $2,000.

In May 1983, the world premiere of a documentary film on Richard Wawro's life was held. The film, produced by Dr. Laurence Becker of Austin, Texas, was titled *With Eyes Wide Open* and has won a number of awards internationally. As Becker said of Richard and his art in the documentary:

"To walk into a room at an exhibition; and to be surrounded by Richard's pictures is to share in his search for the light. To join, even briefly with him and to look at a new kind of world through the eyes of one who receives his gift of sight, severely limited though it may be, with eyes wide open, is to rejoice and be glad that his eyes have enabled us to see so much more clearly than we ever imagined before the beauty and wonder in the ordinary world which daily surrounds us."6

Though in some ways they were similar, the lives of Nadia and Richard Wawro differ sharply. Like Nadia, Richard had an extremely limited use of language. In fact, he hardly spoke until he was 11 and his language skills remain less than ideal today. It is significant to note, however, that as Richard's ability to use language improved, unlike Nadia, his artistic gifts did not suffer. On the contrary, both language and art seemed to be enhanced in the young man with time and training. In addition, it may be of interest to note that, like Nadia, Richard also lost his mother. He had enjoyed a close and loving relationship with her, but her death did not diminish his artistic ability in any way. Why do such circumstances seem to directly affect the talent of one savant and not another? There are still no definite answers.

Another special skill exhibited by autistic savants is musical ability. One such extremely talented musician is Tony DeBlois. Besides being autistic, DeBlois is blind.

Born three months prematurely, he weighed less than 2 pounds (0.9 kilogram) at birth. Tony's mother, Janice DeBlois, was determined to do all she could to help her child. She continuously looked for new items or activities that might interest or stimulate him and it was through one of these that she discovered Tony's musical capacity. She recalled:

"When he was two, because he wasn't walking yet, I decided to get a Magnus chord organ at a garage sale. I took the legs off it, and sat it down on the floor. I wanted to give him encouragement to be able to sit up. One day I heard him. And he put the three notes of 'Twinkle, Twinkle, Little Star' together and I ran in there and I showed him the rest of it, and he was able to pick it right up, and do it."[7]

As time passed, Tony's talent seemed to flower. He was able to play more challenging pieces and was beginning to be seen as a very special musical child. When her son was about nine years old, Janice moved from South Dakota to Massachusetts so that Tony would be able to attend the Perkins School for the Blind. She thought he would be able to get the best training there but, before long, she began having concerns regarding the direction her son's education was taking. "When they gave me a report on Tony," she related, "that said that he was doing 5 percent of what the, quote, normal blind child was doing, I'm going, 'Why are you teaching him to put nuts and bolts together in a workshop when he was already making $50 an hour as a musician?' It doesn't make sense."[8]

Getting advanced musical training for Tony was not going to be automatic or easy despite his obvious talent. His mother had to go to court to convince Perkins and the state that her son would not profit from the typical vocational training given to blind or autistic young people. She felt it was a waste of state funding to continue on that path and insisted that someone with Tony's musical talent would be best off at the highly acclaimed Berklee College of Music in Boston. Apparently Ms. DeBlois' reasoning was persuasive because that's where Tony wound up.

Of course, Janice DeBlois also had to convince Berklee that her son would be an apt pupil. "[The college would ask me] how do you then, teach somebody who can't read, who can't write, and who can hardly speak?" she recalled. "[I'd tell them] you teach it to Tony, and you have him show you concretely on the piano what he's learned."9

Professor Susanna Shifter, Tony's piano teacher at Berklee, soon saw that Janice DeBlois was right. She explained: "I couldn't give him a piece of music and have him read that, so I would have to play something for him. So that was the real difference in teaching him, that absolutely everything he learned, I had to play."10 His teacher went on to explain how finding a common ground with others through music helped Tony get past some of the communication obstacles that autism imposes.

"When he [Tony] came to Berklee, music was his language, and through music, he got to know other people. So because we were all musicians with him, we were talking to him on his level. That helped him to come out a lot because he was able to relate to a lot more people that way."11

Tony graduated from Berklee in 1998 with honors. While his ability as a jazz musician is outstanding, he has also mastered other musical styles including classical and country. In all, Tony DeBlois now plays 14 musical instruments. His inspiring life story was the subject of a CBS Movie of the Week—*Journey to the Heart* that aired in March 1999. Tony DeBlois has also been a guest on a number of television shows and made frequent media appearances. His mother, who is tremendously proud of Tony, gives her son all the credit for his success. "I've opened the doors for Tony," she said, "but it's been him who proudly walks through."[12]

Anxious to learn more about savant musical ability, British researchers John Sloboda, Beate Hermelia, and Neil O'Connor of London conducted a study involving a 23-year-old autistic savant known as N.P. This musically talented young man had lived in a residential home for the disabled since his late teens. Like many people with autism, N.P. was hesitant to make eye contact, had severely limited language abilities, and was socially withdrawn.

Yet N.P.'s gift for music was obvious. By the time he was 21, he was an accomplished pianist and also played the guitar and recorder. He had given concerts and his music was well received. N.P.'s music repertoire largely consisted of tunes he had heard only once or twice before.

The researchers compared N.P.'s musical ability with that of a musical prodigy of normal intelligence who was not autistic. They had hoped to learn more about savant skills, but at the end of the study concluded that there was still much they did not know. The researchers confessed that they couldn't explain how N.P. learned to play the piano or the other instruments. They were also unsure why such considerable musical ability developed in someone who otherwise functioned at a fairly low level. The researchers did observe and note the following: "When we look at the memory capacity of N.P. [or the musical prodigy of normal intelligence], and possibly Mozart, we are looking at essentially the same phenomenon."[13] However, while acknowledging the impressive structure and accuracy of N.P.'s music, the research team realized that his playing lacked expression or feeling and tended to have a "wooden" or rigid quality to it.

Scientists are not sure how savants acquire their miraculous abilities. Theories exist about why these spots of genius appear in many individuals who are seriously challenged in most other areas, but nothing has been proved conclusively. At this point, some research suggests that savant skills are a result of compensation in the right portion of the brain for damage in the brain's left hemisphere. Researchers suspect that other factors are at work as well, but as the British team found out, this remains an area in need of further investigation.

Not every autistic savant becomes famous or involved in research studies. For some, their abilities are too isolated and their other problems too great for them to find gainful employment. That was the challenge for Dolly Montague's sister Henrietta Giardini. Henrietta is an autistic savant with a remarkable memory and an uncanny ability for calendar calculations. She can tell you the precise date a photograph was taken by merely looking at it.

Henrietta is also talented musically. Her mother, who was a South Boston music teacher, had kept Henrietta's crib near a grand piano when she gave music lessons. Though no one is able to explain how it happened, Henrietta began humming operatic arias long before she managed to say her first word. She can also play any tune on the piano after hearing it only once.

As a child, Dolly had formed a special bond with her sister and in many ways became her protector. She knew that Henrietta's savant skills were a source of pride to her sister but they were of little use in helping Henrietta earn a living. Dolly was determined to help turn things around for her sister, but it was 1944—a time when most autistic and mentally retarded people were placed in institutions rather than on jobs.

Dolly decided to try anyway. She brought nineteen-year-old Henrietta to Beth Israel Hospital in Boston, hoping to persuade the personnel department to hire her sister. In return for giving Henrietta a chance to work in their kitchen, Dolly offered to work alongside her for free. That way she believed she could train Henrietta to perform the necessary tasks to keep the job. The hospital decided to give the idea a try, but Dolly did not have to work for free. Both sisters were hired and put on the payroll!

Henrietta's savant memory skills not only allow her to recall the day, date, and time she started on the job but also what the weather was like that day—and every other day that week! She said, "June 6, Tuesday morning at 8:30 I started. 1944. It was a nice day. Tuesday, Wednesday, Thursday, Friday, increasing cloudiness, and Saturday was a cloudy day. I worked from Tuesday to Saturday and off Sunday."[14]

Ironically, the work Henrietta was hired to do was ideal for an autistic individual. Most autistic people of

Henrietta's intelligence level do best in situations where the tasks are clearly defined and somewhat regimented. Henrietta's job was to place the correct food on plates in a certain order. The job seemed tailor-made for her and Henrietta rose to the occasion in performing it. Her sister Dolly described the situation this way: "[Her] hands were like, well, they were useful hands, and so they were well coordinated. She was faster than even other workers that were around there but what I had to teach her was how to behave, how not to bark like a dog if she felt like it or imitate people."[15]

Dolly worked with Henrietta in the hospital kitchen for about a year. By then, Henrietta was fully able to handle the job and its responsibilities alone. She showed herself to be an able and dependable worker and remained on the hospital's kitchen staff most of the next 46 years. In 1990, when Henrietta turned 65, she retired. She was given a retirement party by her friends and coworkers, and even the president of Beth Israel Hospital attended to honor her.

It was also an important moment for Dolly—the family member who had been so determined to help her sister find a meaningful place in society. "All my life I felt guilty enjoying the things that most people do enjoy," Dolly confessed. "I went to proms. I graduated. I knew what it was to be the star of the day when I was a bride. I had children and I pondered often, pondered about how Henrietta missed out on all those kinds of things and what I could do to make it up to her. I wanted Henrietta to feel the pride and dignity, all the great things that come out of being a star."[16]

Henrietta was the star on the night of her retirement party. She wore a corsage and received heartfelt congratulations from a large group of people who had come to know her and respect what she had accomplished. As the hospital spokesperson told Henrietta at the party, "On behalf of thousands of people, the grateful hospital extends its warm thanks and best wishes upon your retirement. Congratulations."[17]

Henrietta also provided a special surprise for her coworkers—many of whom had not known about her musical ability. Dolly announced her sister's intention, saying: "Henrietta has graciously consented to entertain us at the piano with a few selections she has chosen. She would like to dedicate her first number to the Beth Israel Hospital [staff] which will be *"Nom Peace Verdad de Meir"* which in English means 'Don't Forget Me.'[18]

It was a wonderful evening filled with joy and pride. Dolly had successfully shown that someone like her sister can have a valued place in society and Henrietta, through her years of service at the hospital, had proved that Dolly was right. Dolly described how she felt about her special sister this way, "Henrietta's my inspiration, my teacher, my mentor, my best friend, and I always take pride in saying Henrietta's my sister."[19]

CHAPTER SEVEN
Today and Tomorrow

NOT LONG AGO the prognosis for an autistic child was dismal. Neither the medical profession nor the general public understood this disorder, and many of these young people were wrongly labeled "stupid" or "insane." It was rare for an autistic child to receive help early on and eventually be mainstreamed into the community. Fortunately, through the years, many important advances have been made and as the Autism Society of America says, "With appropriate services, training, and information, [today] most families are able to support their son or daughter at home."[1]

While keeping the family intact can greatly enhance the quality of life for everyone involved, the families of autistic children are frequently under considerable stress. These parents, as well as the brothers and sisters, have to contend with the sometimes exasperating behavior of the affected family member. Although they understand what their loved one is going through, others around them may not, and this has caused some painfully awkward situations. At times, an autistic child's difficulties have prevented the family from fully participating in community activities they might enjoy. The result is that some family members are left feeling more cut off and alone than ever.

Parents sometimes feel that securing all the necessary services and treatments an autistic child needs can be a full-time job, and in some instances, this places a

The Sherman family moved to Lawrence, Kansas, so that three-year-old Sammy could enroll in the school district's noted autism program.

financial strain on the family too. When one or both parents become overly involved with a special-needs child, other children in the family may feel neglected. Resentments can build up which no one involved feels prepared to deal with. To handle these difficulties, families need effective coping strategies.

The suggestions below are based on the experiences of families in dealing with autism and on NIMH-sponsored studies of effective ways to handle stress:

Work as a family. In times of stress, family members tend to take their frustrations out on each other when they most need mutual support. Despite the difficulties in finding child care, couples find that taking breaks without their children helps renew their bonds. The other children also need attention, and need to have a voice in expressing and solving problems.

Keep a sense of humor. Parents find that the ability to laugh and say, "You won't believe what our child has done now!" helps them maintain a healthy sense of perspective.

Notice progress. When it seems that all the help, love, and support is going nowhere, it's important to remember that, over time, real progress is being made. Families are better able to maintain their hope if they celebrate the small signs of growth and change they see.

Take action. Many parents gain strength working with others on behalf of all children with autism. Working to win additional resources, community programs, or school services helps parents see themselves as important contributors to the well-being of others as well as of their own child.

Plan ahead. Naturally, most parents want to know that when they die, their offspring will be safe and cared for. Having a plan in place helps relieve some of the worry. Some parents form a contract with a professional guardian, who agrees to look after the interests of the person with autism, such as observing birthdays and arranging for care.[2]

In addition, many support groups for both the parents and siblings of autistic individuals help families deal with this problem and feel less alone. People who've gone through similar experiences can often offer empathy as well as useful advice.

Families can also look forward to the important strides in research that have been achieved in recent years. The National Institute of Neurological Disorders and Stroke and the National Institute of Mental Health support research studies aimed at identifying the brain abnormalities underlying autism. And, in May 1997, the National Institute on Deafness and Other Communication Disorders (NIDCD) and the National Institute of Child Health and Human Development (NICHD) launched a five-year collaborative effort to learn how autism develops. The undertaking involves more than 65 scientists from 24 universities throughout the world. Among the countries participating are the United States, Canada, France, and Britain.

To learn more about the brain of autistic individuals, researchers are now using new methods of brain imaging, as well as other innovative and exploratory techniques. These allow scientists to see the human brain in action. They are able to observe and more fully understand the changes that occur in the brain when a person lifts a glass, for example, or carries on a conversation, or adds and subtracts. Through such techniques, researchers may be able to learn precisely what areas of the brain are involved when specific tasks are performed. One such study specifically looks at malfunctioning brain circuits associated with impaired thinking about human relationships—a problem autistic people face. Other work is being done to find out more about how different parts of the brain function in relation to one another and how changes occurring in these areas in the developing fetus may result in autism.

Various aspects of autistic behavior are also being studied to enable scientists to see how such behaviors differ from those of other children. They hope to find out more about how autistic children process information. Research is being done on the communication problems faced by autistic individuals as well. Scientists are exploring the effect of certain drugs on the autistic individual's ability to communicate. Studying speech and language in this manner helps health-care professionals to evaluate current treatment methods and design better ones.

Because heredity is believed to play a role in autism, some important genetic research is underway. Valuable information has been acquired from studies using postmortem brain tissue (brain tissue removed after a person has died). With access to the brain tissue of autistic individuals, scientists may be better able to pinpoint any abnormal gene activity within cells. Being able to identify irregular genes could also eventually lead to earlier diagnoses and more effective treatment programs. Further gene research is also being done to gain insight into the possible connection between autism and the other brain disorders that sometimes occur with it.

To meet the demand for brain tissue, the National Institute of Mental Health has worked with patient groups and other institutes to establish brain-bank collections for the study of autism. Among these is the Harvard Brain Tissue Center, which strives to amass this vital resource as well to ensure its availability to scientists in the field. Usually, families anxious to help others arrange for the tissue donations upon the death of a relative with autism.

Hopefully, these government-sponsored research programs will one day make an important difference. As the National Institute of Mental Health expressed its goal: "Ultimately the results of NIMH's extensive research program may translate into better lives for people with autism. . . . Someday, we may even have the ability to prevent the disorder. Perhaps researchers will learn to identify children at risk for autism at birth, allowing doctors and other health-care professionals to begin preventive therapy before symptoms ever develop. Or, as scientists learn more about the genetic transmission of autism, they may be able to replace any defective genes before the infant is even born."[3]

An important step in this direction came in May 2000. National Institutes of Health researchers indicated that they had uncovered heightened levels of key brain proteins in the blood of newborns who later became autistic. This could mean that a biological marker for the disorder may have been discovered. If this is so, children with it could be identified and perhaps even treated before autism's symptoms surface.

In addition to government-sponsored research, private organizations have also done a great deal to enhance the public's knowledge of autism and stimulate further research on various aspects of the disorder. Among these is the Autism Society of America, which

Junior high softball player Anna Inskip, who is autistic, won her right to play on her school team because of the Americans with Disabilities Act.

established the Autism Society of America Foundation (ASAF) "to raise and allocate funds for research and to address the many unanswered questions about autism."[4]

Besides its encouraging work in other areas, the ASAF has explored the societal and economic consequences of autism on families and endeavored to develop a registry of individuals and families willing to participate in research studies. The Foundation has also raised large sums for biomedical research to explore enhanced treatment approaches to autism.

Every summer, the Autism Society of America holds a national conference that provides an important opportunity for information-gathering as well as networking for people concerned about this disorder.

Often more than 2,000 people attend the conference and have access to a range of presentations and seminars regarding autism. The Autism Society also has more than 240 chapters in 50 states that provide support services on a state and local level. In addition, many other private organizations offer help to autistic individuals and their families and are actively involved in the fight against autism.

At times, that fight overflows from the medical and research arena into the political realm. The Cure Autism Now (CAN) Foundation is a nonprofit organization of parents, physicians, and researchers dedicated to promoting and funding research with direct clinical implications for treatment and a cure for autism. CAN had been extremely active in gathering grass-roots support for the Children's Health Bill (HR 3301) and summarized what this vital legislation would do as follows:

- **Create up to five Centers for Excellence for autism**. These university sites would combine clinical and basic research in autism, draw the attention of the nation's top scientists, and exist as part of a network that enables findings to be rapidly disseminated and replicated. This exact approach has been very effective in Alzheimer's and childhood leukemia.

- **Establish at least three Centers of Expertise on autism epidemiology at the Centers for Disease Control (CDC)**. These centers will assist states in creating surveillance programs to track cases of autism and identify trends. This is very important right now as there is a growing sense that the incidence of autism is on the rise.

- **Create a centralized and open facility for gene- and brain-banking**. These are essential for scientific progress in autism.

- **Develop an awareness campaign for the public and physicians**. Greater awareness means earlier diagnosis. . . . Currently, physicians often do not understand autism or know how to diagnose it, thus losing valuable months, and sometimes years, of potentially critical treatment in many cases.

- **Legislate roughly $40 million a year for five years to autism**. This more than doubles the amount the NIH now spends on autism research.

- **Bring together the resources** of the National Institutes of Health (NIH), the Centers for Disease Control (CDC) and the Department of Health and Human Services (DHHS) to attack the problem of autism.[5]

Television star Anthony Edwards poses outside the Ed Sullivan Theater in New York to promote CAN (Cure Autism Now). He was appearing on the Late Show *with David Letterman.*

On September 14, 1999, Anthony Edwards, star of the television show *ER*, testified before the Senate in favor of the bill. He stated: "I am speaking on behalf of the 400,000 families in the U.S., and in particular for the hundreds of families I have come to know as I have worked with the Cure Autism Now Foundation over the past 2 years.

"Here are the statistics, the dry stuff that isn't supposed to make you cry. Autism affects at least 1 in 500 kids. That's more than multiple sclerosis or Down's syndrome or cystic fibrosis. That's at least 400,000 people in the United States. It strikes children, generally between their first and second birthdays. These kids will live as long as you or me. But their parents will not be experiencing slumber parties, graduations, and weddings in June. . . .

"This is how a mother I know put it—sometime before her son's second birthday, someone crept into her house and took her precious baby's mind and personality and left his bewildered body behind. If 1 in 500 kids were actually being abducted in the United States, it would be a national emergency and so should this be.

"And that's why I'm here today.

"In the 1950's, when scientists first started describing autism, it was the heyday of psychoanalysis. Scientists blamed autism on bad parenting, trauma, refrigerator mothers. Because of this tragic mistake, parents were stigmatized. Parents never organized, serious scientists did no research, and a generation of children was lost to medical progress.

"We are not asking you to tell the NIH how to do the science, what to fund, and what not. We're asking you to create a policy that says 'do some science for God's sake.' Take advantage of what is known and use it. That is why we are asking for centers.

"Parents with autistic children don't know where to get services, they often don't even get a proper diagnosis. Researchers can't get access to families and that slows down progress. This bill creates sites where families can come for diagnosis and clinical care and where the very best scientists can get access to those families. It creates a structure that encourages—no, actually mandates—scientists to work collaboratively, sharing information and treatment protocols.

"This is basically the same model that worked in childhood leukemia. As new treatments were discovered they were tested and validated and refined across collaborative sites. The result—the survival rate for pediatric leukemia has gone from 20 percent to 60 percent. This same center-based approach has helped scientists make major discoveries in Alzheimer's and new treatments are clearly on the horizon.

"It's not only the centers, but it is the money, and let me explain why this may be a special case. In other diseases—breast cancer, prostate cancer, Parkinson's—eventually, sooner rather than later, you die. If you have any money, you leave some to fund research.

"But autism affects children. They don't lobby, they have no voice, they don't raise any money. And their parents are too busy taking care of a very ill child to do much of anything else. When the parents die, if there is any money in the family, it goes toward taking care of the adult children so they don't become wards of the state. The pot never gets any bigger.

"Recently, as the numbers have increased, as famous people like Dan Marino and Doug Flutie and Senator Slade Gorton have come forward to talk about their kids and their grandkids, the autism community has mobilized. They have aggressively recruited scientists, raised money, started resources and fellowships. They feel that the potential to make a breakthrough is here. Despite financial strain and limited time and endless heartbreak, they have done more than their part. Now they are asking you to do yours. . . .

*Buffalo Bills quarterback Doug Flutie, whose son has autism,
meets reporters in Washington to support legislation for autism
research.*

"I know one little boy with autism pretty well. He likes to jump on the trampoline, and play in the sand and sometimes he runs up to you and gives you a hug. But other times, when he is crying late at night, he can't tell his parents if he had a bad dream, a tummy ache, or if he's sad because his little two-year-old brother can talk and he can't—even though he's seven. But when I look into his sparkly brown eyes, I know that they are in there, and that he is in there, and that he's counting on us to help him get out."[6]

Edwards' voice, along with the voices of thousands of others, was finally heard. Autistic individuals and their families won a tremendous victory. After having passed in the U.S. House and U.S. Senate, President Bill Clinton signed the Children's Health Act of 2000 into law on October 17, 2000. Autism would now be seen as a national health priority.

While vital autism research efforts are currently underway, many groups and individuals have also been actively striving for enhanced legislation to bolster the rights of those in the disabled community. They believe it is crucial that national legislators and government agencies be aware of the unique needs of people with autism so that they can make better decisions.

Yet despite laws that have been passed and services that are supposedly in place, the parents of autistic children are still often forced to fight for the services their children are entitled to. That's what happened in West Virginia when the mother of a 14-year-old autistic boy named Matt tried to improve the quality of her son's education. The boy's mother had complained that most of the teachers who worked with Matt lacked the qualifications and experience necessary to do the best job. She noted that often they were university students who went on to better jobs after graduation. In one instance, nearly a whole year was wasted when one of Matt's teachers, who was unfamiliar with his skills and abilities, insisted that he spend months learning the alphabet. That meant Matt would learn nothing since he was already a good reader.

"I know money is tight, but a lot of things can be done with the money that is available," Matt's mother emphasized. "A good learning atmosphere, qualified teachers, and trained personnel are not too much to ask for."[7] Her feelings were underscored by Ruth Sullivan, director of the Autism Services Center, who feels that Matt's experience is not an isolated incident. "Every child is a book, yet every story is the same," she said. "They couldn't get a good diagnosis, and then they couldn't get services. It's literally a fight to get the services."[8]

That fight isn't just an ongoing battle to be waged by autistic people and their families—it's more than the fight of disabled people as well. If we want to live in a society where people receive what they need to reach their full potential, it must be everyone's fight.

End Notes

CHAPTER ONE

1. National Institute of Mental Health, *Autism* (booklet) NIH Publications No. 97-4023, September 1997, p. 4.

CHAPTER TWO

1. Laura Schreibman, *Autism*, Newbury Park, Calif.: Sage Publications, 1988, p. 14.
2. Diana McLellan, "Andrew Awakes," *Ladies Home Journal*, October 1999, p. 102.
3. Gary B. Mesibov, Lynn W. Adams and Laura G. Klinger, *Autism: Understanding the Disorder*, New York: Plenum Press, 1997, p. 3.
4. Oliver Sacks, *An Anthropologist on Mars*, New York: Alfred A. Knopf, 1995, p. 251.
5. Nina M. Riccio, "Understanding Autism," *Current Health*, December 1999, p. 28.
6. National Institute of Mental Health, p. 4.
7. Ruth C. Sullivan, "Autism: Definition Past and Present," *Journal of Vocational Rehabilitation*, January 1994, p. 6.8
8. National Institute of Mental Health, p. 11.

9. Laura Schreibman, p. 19.
10. National Institute of Mental Health, p. 15.
11. Linda-Lynn Fagan, "Autism: Talking in a World Without Language," *JAMA (The Journal of the American Medical Association)*, February 7, 1996, p. 417.
12. Joseph P. Shapiro, "Beyond the Rain Man: A Singular Woman Changes the Cattle Industry and Our Image of Autism," *U.S. News & World Report*, May 25, 1996, p. 78.
13. National Institute of Mental Health, p. 15.
14. Ibid.
15. Ibid., p. 7.
16. National Institute of Neurological Disorders and Stroke. Autism (booklet), NIH Publication No. 95-1877. Unpaged.

CHAPTER THREE
1. Gary B. Mesibov, Lynn W. Adams, and Laura G. Klinger, p. 5.
2. Jean-Marc Itard, *The Wild Boy of Aveyron*, Englewood Cliffs, N.J.: Prentice Hall, 1962, p. 54.
3. Laura Schreibman, p. 13.
4. Autism Society of America, "What Is Autism?" (booklet), January 1999, unpaged.
5. National Organization for Rare Disorders, Autism leaflet, December 13, 1999.
6. National Institute of Mental Health, p. 24.
7. Arthur Allen, "Why Are the Children Sick?" *Redbook*, November 1999, p. 150.

CHAPTER FOUR
1. National Institute of Mental Health, p. 32.

2. "Giant Steps for Autistic Kids: Play Therapy Helps Children Overwhelmed by Sounds and Touch," *MacLeans*, October 5, 1998, p. 66.
3. National Institute of Mental Health, p. 34.
4. Ibid.
5. NIDCD, Fact Sheet, "Communication in Autism." NIH Publication No. 99-4315, October 1998.
6. Nina M. Ricco, "Understanding Autism," *Current Health 2*, December 1999, p. 2.
7. Ibid.
8. National Institute of Mental Health, p. 33.
9. Ibid., p. 38.
10. Ibid., p. 40.
11. Karen Garloch, "Secretin Treatment Offers Hope to Parents of Autistic Children," *Knight-Ridder/ Tribune News Service*, February 22, 1999, p. K5074.
12. National Institute of Neurological Disorders and Stroke.
13. MSNBC TV News—Special Edition, "Could New Therapy Cure Autism?" October 7, 1998, (transcript).
14. Ibid.
15. Ibid.
16. Ibid.
17. Ibid.
18. Ibid.
19. Karen Garloch.
20. Ibid.
21. Ibid.
22. Ibid.
23. Ibid.
24. Shanker Vedantam, "Parents of Autistic Children Are Pinning Their Hopes on Secretin," *Knight-*

Ridder/Tribune News Service, April 12, 1999, p. K6963.

25. Ibid.
26. Ibid.
27. Ibid.
28. Bernard Rimland, "Secretin: Positive, Negative Reports in the 'Top' of the First Inning," *Autism Research Review International*, Vol. 13, No. 4, 1999, p. 7.
29. Ibid.

CHAPTER FIVE

1. Oliver Sacks, p. 246.
2. Marilyn Larkin, "Approaches to Amelioration in Autism in Adulthood," *The Lancet*, January 18, 1997, p. 186.
3. Ibid.
4. Ibid.
5. Jeanne Kennedy, "They're Under One Roof, but Leading Separate Lives," *The Herald Dispatcher*, April 3, 1992, p. 12.
6. National Institute of Mental Health, p. 30.
7. "Blue-collaring It in Rockville: People with Autism Working." From the President's Committee on Employment of the Handicapped, 1983/4, p. 12.
8. Ibid.
9. Ibid.
10. Ibid.
11. National Institute of Mental Health, p. 46.
12. "Blue Collaring It in Rockville," p. 12.
13. National Institute of Mental Health, p. 46.
14. Oliver Sacks, p. 247.
15. Ibid., p. 254.

16. Temple Grandin and Margaret M. Scarino, *Emergence: Labeled Autistic*, New York: Warner Books, 1986, p. 18.
17. Ibid., p. 20.
18. Ibid., p. 21.
19. Oliver Sacks, p. 255.
20. Ibid., p. 265.
21. Ibid., p. 259.
22. Ibid., p. 261.
23. Ibid., p. 272.
24. Ibid., p. 291.
25. Ibid., p. 292.
26. Ibid., p. 296.
27. Gary H. Anthes, "Computer Savants: For the Autistic, the Binary World of Computing Can Be a Place to Excel," *Computer World*, April 14, 1997, p. 95.
28. Gary H. Anthes, "Autistics in the Workplace." *Computer World*, April 14, 1997, Online.
29. Gary H. Anthes, "Computer savants."
30. Gary H. Anthes, "Autistics in the Workplace."
31. Gary H. Anthes, "Computer savants."
32. Ibid.

CHAPTER SIX

1. Schreibman, Laura, p. 25.
2. Darold Treffert, M.D., *Extraordinary People: Understanding Idiot Savants*. New York: Harper & Row, 1988, p. 80.
3. Oliver Sacks, p. 195.
4. Darold Treffert, p. 81.
5. Ibid., p. 89.
6. Ibid., p. 91.

7. *Sunday Morning* (television show), "In His Hands," March 2, 1997 (transcript).

8. Ibid.

9. Ibid.

10. Ibid.

11. Ibid.

12. Ibid.

13. Darold A. Treppert, p. 30.

14. *20/20* (television show), November 9, 1990 (transcript).

15. Ibid.

16. Ibid.

17. Ibid.

18. Ibid.

19. Ibid.

CHAPTER SEVEN

1. Autism Society of America, "What Is Autism?"

2. National Institute of Mental Health, pp. 48–49.

3. National Institute of Mental Health, p. 51.

4. Autism Society of America, "What is Autism?"

5. The Cure Autism Now Foundation, Political Action Alert!, March 27, 2000, Online.

6. Testimony of Anthony Edwards to the Senate, September 14, 1999, The Cure Autism Now Foundation, Online.

7. Jeanne Kennedy, "A Fight on Two Fronts: Families Battle the Disorder and Struggle for Services. *The Herald Dispatch*, (Huntington, West Virginia), April 3, 1992, p. 1.

8. Ibid.

For Further Reading

Barron, J. and S. Barron. *There's a Boy in Here*. New York: Simons and Schuster, 1992.

Gold, P. *Please Don't Say Hello*. New York: Human Science Press/Plenum Publications, 1986.

Grandin, T. *Thinking In Pictures and Other Reports from My Life with Autism*. New York: Doubleday, 1995.

Grandin, T. *Emergence: Labeled Autistic*. Novato, Calif.: Arena Press, 1966.

Hart, C. *Without Reason: A Family Copes with Two Generations of Autism*. New York: Harper & Row, 1989.

Sacks, Oliver. *An Anthropologist on Mars*. New York: Alfred A. Knopf, 1995.

William, D. *Somebody Somewhere*. New York: Times Books, 1994.

Organizations Concerned with Autism

American Association of University Affiliated Programs
for Persons with Developmental Disabilities (AAUAP)
8630 Fenton Street, Suite 410
Silver Spring, MD 20910

American Speech-Language-Hearing Association
10801 Rockville Pike
Rockville, MD 20852

The Association of Persons with Severe Handicaps
(TASH)
29 West Susquehanna Avenue, Suite 210
Baltimore, MD 21304

The Autism National Committee
635 Ardmore Avenue
Ardmore, PA 19003

Autism Network for Dietary Intervention
P.O. Box 17711
Rochester, NY 14617-0711

Autism Network for Hearing and Visually Impaired Persons
7510 Ocean Front Avenue
Virginia Beach, VA 23451

Autism Research Institute
4182 Adams Avenue
San Diego, CA 92116

Autism Society of America, Inc.
7910 Woodmont Avenue, Suite 650
Bethesda, MD 20814

The Beach Center on Families and Disability
3111 Haworth Hall
University of Kansas
Lawrence, KA 66045

Council for Exceptional Children
11920 Association Drive
Reston, VA 20191-1589

Cure Autism Now (CAN)
5225 Wilshire Boulevard, Suite 503
Los Angeles, CA 90036

Department of Education
Office of Special Education Programs
330 C Street SW
Mail Stop 2651
Washington, DC 20202

Federation of Families for Children's Mental
Health
1021 Prince Street
Alexandria, VA 22314

Indiana Resource Center on Autism
Institute for the Study of Developmental Disabilities
Indiana University
2853 East Tenth Street
Bloomington, IN 47408-2601

National Alliance for Autism Research
414 Wall Street, Research Park
Princeton, NJ 08540

National Information Center for Children and Youth
with Disabilities (NICDCY)
P.O. Box 1492
Washington, DC 20013-1492

NATIONAL INSTITUTES OF HEALTH
Agencies that sponsor research on autism and related
disorders
www.nih.gov/icd

National Institute of Child Health and Human Development (NICHD)
31 Center Drive
Bldg. 31, Rm. 2A-32
Bethesda, MD 20892
(301) 496-5133 (Voice)
(301) 496-7101 (Fax)
www.nichd.nih.gov (Internet)

National Institute on Deafness and Other Communication Disorders (NIDCD)
31 Center Drive
Bldg. 31, Rm. 3C-31
Bethesda, MD 20892
(301) 496-7243 (Voice)
(301) 402-0018 (Fax)
www.nidcd.nih.gov (Internet)

National Institute of Mental Health (NIMH)
5600 Fishers Lane
Parklawn Bldg. Rm. 7C02
Rockville, MD 20857-8030
(301) 443-4513 (Voice)
(301) 443-0008 (Fax)
www.nimh.nih.gov (Internet)

National Institute of Neurological Disorders and Stroke (NINDS)
31 Center Drive
Bldg. 31, Rm. 8A-06
Bethesda, MD 20892
(301) 496-5924 (Voice)
(301) 402-2186 (Fax)
www.ninds.nih.gov (Internet)

Index